100 Poems to Live By

POETIC REMEDIES FOR ANY OCCASION

JOSEPH PIERCY

Michael O'Mara Books Limited

First published in Great Britain in 2026 by
Michael O'Mara Books Limited
9 Lion Yard
Tremadoc Road
London SW4 7NQ

EU representative:
Authorised Rep Compliance Ltd
Ground Floor, 71 Baggot Street Lower
Dublin D02 P593
Ireland

Copyright © Michael O'Mara Books 2026

All rights reserved. You may not copy, store, distribute, transmit, reproduce or otherwise make available this publication (or any part of it) in any form, or by any means (electronic, digital, optical, mechanical, photocopying, recording, machine readable, text/data mining or otherwise), without the prior written permission of the publisher. Any person who does any unauthorized act in relation to this publication may be liable to criminal prosecution and civil claims for damages.

Every reasonable effort has been made to acknowledge all copyright holders. Any errors or omissions that may have occurred are inadvertent, and anyone with any copyright queries is invited to write to the publisher, so that a full acknowledgement may be included in subsequent editions of this work.

A CIP catalogue record for this book is available from the British Library.

This product is made of material from well-managed, FSC®-certified forests and other controlled sources. The manufacturing processes conform to the environmental regulations of the country of origin.

For further information see
www.mombooks.com/about/sustainability-climate-focus
Report any safety issues to product.safety@mombooks.com and see www.mombooks.com/contact/product-safety

UK editions:
ISBN: 978-1-78929-834-5 in hardback print format
ISBN: 978-1-78929-835-2 in ebook format

US editions:
ISBN: 978-1-78929-886-4 in hardback print format
ISBN: 978-1-78929-914-4 in ebook format

1 2 3 4 5 6 7 8 9 10

Cover design by Claire Cater, using illustrations from Shutterstock
Designed and typeset by Barbara Ward
Printed and bound by CPI Group (UK) Ltd, Croydon, CR0 4YY

www.mombooks.com

Contents

Introduction 4

1. Remedies for the Heart 7

2. Remedies for the Soul and Spirit 49

3. Remedies for the Mind 89

4. Remedies for the Self and Others 131

5. Remedies for Everyday Living 175

List of Poets and Poems 219

Acknowledgements 221

Credits 221

Introduction

Poetry exists in the liminal space between those fragile, luminous moments where language transcends mere communication and becomes pure emotion, pure experience. This anthology is a testament to that transformative power, a gathering of voices that whisper, shout, tremble and soar across the landscapes of human consciousness.

The Victorian critic and poet Matthew Arnold defined poetry as 'The criticism of life under the conditions fixed for such criticism by the laws of poetic truth and poetic beauty'. Within these pages, you will find not just poems, but living landscapes: intimate geographies of emotion, mapped by writers who dare to explore the uncharted territories of feeling. Although the poems are attached to a stated 'condition or situation', these are afflictions of the heart and mind and not illnesses (apart from love sickness, of which there is plenty on show). Each poem is a cartography of a certain vulnerability of emotion, a precise rendering of a moment, a sensitivity and a fleeting truth that might otherwise dissolve into silence.

In times of struggle or uncertainty, we often turn to words for solace. The pages that follow honour this timeless tradition by bringing together poems whose lines can resonate with the hope and resilience of the human spirit. In each instance, we catch glimpses of hard-won insights forged in pain, as well as gentle moments of quiet reflection. These verses serve as witnesses to our most exposed experiences, reminding us that empathy can thrive when we name our truths.

During life's challenges, poetry can be both a refuge and a catalyst for growth. It allows us to slow down, to breathe in every syllable, and to find meaning in the most ordinary moments. When the complexities of grief, depression or fear feel all-consuming, poems guide us to discover new languages for what we feel – words that help unravel knots in our hearts and illuminate hidden corners of our souls.

The poems are drawn from across the globe, traversing centuries, cultures, epochs and religions. Poetry, often seen as highbrow or inaccessible within some appraisals of Western cultures, is viewed very differently in other countries and societies, where the poet is often seen to give voice to the voiceless and oppressed. What unites every poet in this collection is not a single style, point of view or aesthetic, but a commitment to authenticity, to rendering the world not just as it appears, but as it is deeply, privately felt.

As you journey through this anthology, consider each poem an invitation to explore the transformative power of expression. Let the language wash over you, comfort and provoke you, perhaps even inspire you to write your own responses in the margins. Allow the cadence of these voices – some ancient, some contemporary – to remind you that healing is not a destination but a compassionate unfolding of soul and self. Throughout history, poetry has been a sanctuary for those seeking solace and understanding. It has the power to transform pain into beauty, to turn isolation into connection, and to illuminate the path from despair to hope. In this collection, we celebrate the resilience of the human spirit and the capacity of words to mend what is broken.

May these poems grant you solace, spark your imagination, or simply remind you that, even in the deepest darkness, a single chord of truth or understanding can launch a powerful shift toward wholeness. Welcome to *100 Poems to Live By*, and to the ever-renewing gift of poetry's healing embrace.

Joseph Piercy

1

Remedies for the Heart

CONDITION OR SITUATION:
Unrequited Love

PRESCRIPTION:
A Leave-Taking (1866)
by Algernon Charles Swinburne

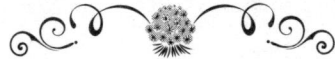

'A Leave-Taking' by Victorian poet Algernon Charles Swinburne is a poem about the painful experience of unrequited love. The poet, consumed by longing for someone who doesn't reciprocate his feelings, contemplates ending his own life by walking into the sea, yet ultimately chooses not to as even an act of extreme self-sacrifice is unlikely to elicit any attention from the object of the poet's ardour.

The poem explores themes of despair, resignation and the futility of love when met with indifference, although the reality of the situation is finally accepted and, with this acceptance, the poet is able to move on with his life.

Let us go hence, my songs; she will not hear.
Let us go hence together without fear;
Keep silence now, for singing-time is over,
And over all old things and all things dear.
She loves not you nor me as all we love her.
Yea, though we sang as angels in her ear,
        She would not hear.

Let us rise up and part; she will not know.
Let us go seaward as the great winds go,
Full of blown sand and foam; what help is here?
There is no help, for all these things are so,
And all the world is bitter as a tear.
And how these things are, though ye strove to show,
    She would not know.

Let us go home and hence; she will not weep.
We gave love many dreams and days to keep,
Flowers without scent, and fruits that would not grow,
Saying, 'If thou wilt, thrust in thy sickle and reap.'
All is reaped now; no grass is left to mow;
And we that sowed, though all we fell on sleep,
    She would not weep.

Let us go hence and rest; she will not love.
She shall not hear us if we sing hereof,
Nor see love's ways, how sore they are and steep.
Come hence, let be, lie still; it is enough.
Love is a barren sea, bitter and deep;
And though she saw all heaven in flower above,
    She would not love.

Let us give up, go down; she will not care.
Though all the stars made gold of all the air,
And the sea moving saw before it move
One moon-flower making all the foam-flowers fair;
Though all those waves went over us, and drove

Deep down the stifling lips and drowning hair,
>   She would not care.

Let us go hence, go hence; she will not see.
Sing all once more together; surely she,
She too, remembering days and words that were,
Will turn a little toward us, sighing; but we,
We are hence, we are gone, as though we had not been there.
Nay, and though all men seeing had pity on me,
>   She would not see.

CONDITION OR SITUATION:
The Unbearable Torment of True Love

PRESCRIPTION:
Restless Love (1776)
by Johann Wolfgang von Goethe

When we think of Romantic poets we often think of the 'big six' English poets, namely Keats, Byron, Shelley, Coleridge, Wordsworth and Blake – all of whom appear in this collection. However, the Romantic Movement was pan-European and the German Romantics certainly knew a thing or two about love.

'Restless Love' by Goethe captures the turbulent nature of passionate love and its relationship to human suffering. The poem's central message is that love is an overwhelming force that brings both joy and torment, driving the poet to constant emotional upheaval. Through weather imagery (wind, rain, snow) and the metaphor of restless movement through nature, Goethe expresses how love creates a state of perpetual unease and yearning. The poet finds himself compelled to move through harsh conditions, suggesting that love forces us to endure hardship and emotional torment willingly. Goethe ultimately realizes that this restless, painful state is inherent in the experience of deep love and is both a blessing and a curse.

Through rain, through snow,
Through tempest go!
'Mongst steaming caves,
O'er misty waves,
On, on! still on!
Peace, rest have flown!

Sooner through sadness
    I'd wish to be slain,
Than all the gladness
    Of life to sustain;
All the fond yearning
    That heart feels for heart,
Only seems burning
    To make them both smart!

How shall I fly?
Forestwards hie?
Vain were all strife!
Bright crown of life,
Turbulent bliss,—
Love, thou art this!

CONDITION OR SITUATION:
Long-Distance Relationships

PRESCRIPTION:
Here I Love You (1924)

by Pablo Neruda

'Here I Love You' by the Chilean poet Pablo Neruda explores themes of love, longing and distance in relationships in deeply emotional and redolent language. The central message revolves around how love persists even when lovers are physically separated. The poem evokes a voice that continues to feel intense love for someone who is absent, emphasizing how love transcends physical space. Through imagery of the night, wind and stars, Neruda illustrates how natural elements become signs, symbols and reminders of the absent lover, both comforting and tormenting for them.

A key theme is the contrast between a lover's presence and absence – while they are physically gone, their presence is felt everywhere in nature and in the speaker's thoughts. The poem also explores the bittersweet aspect of memory and how it keeps love alive while simultaneously highlighting the pain of separation. Neruda's message is that true love continues to exist and remains powerful even when lovers are apart.

Here I love you.
In the dark pines the wind disentangles itself.
The moon glows like phosphorous on the vagrant waters.
Days, all one kind, go chasing each other.

The snow unfurls in dancing figures.
A silver gull slips down from the west.
Sometimes a sail. High, high stars.
Oh the black cross of a ship.
Alone.

Sometimes I get up early and even my soul is wet.
Far away the sea sounds and resounds.
This is a port.

Here I love you.
Here I love you and the horizon hides you in vain.
I love you still among these cold things.
Sometimes my kisses go on those heavy vessels
that cross the sea towards no arrival.
I see myself forgotten like those old anchors.

The piers sadden when the afternoon moors there.
My life grows tired, hungry to no purpose.
I love what I do not have. You are so far.
My loathing wrestles with the slow twilights.
But night comes and starts to sing to me.

The moon turns its clockwork dream.
The biggest stars look at me with your eyes.
And as I love you, the pines in the wind
want to sing your name with their leaves of wire.

CONDITION OR SITUATION:
Leaving It Too Late to Show Feelings

PRESCRIPTION:
Come Not, When I Am Dead (1830)
by Alfred, Lord Tennyson

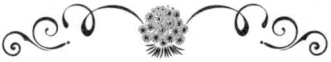

There's no time like the present to speak from the heart before it's too late and things remain unsaid. 'Come Not, When I Am Dead' confronts mortality with a bittersweet awareness that death creates an unbridgeable divide, rendering posthumous grief hollow compared to living connection. Lord Tennyson suggests that genuine love must be expressed in the present – tears shed for the living hold more value than those wasted on the dead, who can no longer receive comfort.

The poem speaks to our human tendency to postpone emotional honesty until it's too late, creating a gentle but urgent reminder that time for meaningful connection is finite. Its message resonates as a plea for emotional authenticity and present-moment appreciation of those we cherish.

Come not, when I am dead,
   To drop thy foolish tears upon my grave,
To trample round my fallen head,
   And vex the unhappy dust thou wouldst not save.
There let the wind sweep, and the plover cry;
     But go thou by.

Child, if it were thine error or thy crime
   I care no longer, being all unblest:
Wed whom thou wilt, but I am sick of Time,
   And I desire to rest.
Pass on, weak heart, and leave to where I lie:
     Go by, go by!

CONDITION OR SITUATION:
The End of a Secret Love Affair

PRESCRIPTION:
When We Two Parted (1816)

by George Gordon, Lord Byron

'When We Two Parted' by Lord Byron is a melancholic exploration of lost love, secret relationships and lingering emotional pain. The poem captures the aftermath of a forbidden romance that ended in silence and shame, likely inspired by one of Byron's own affairs with a married woman (of which there were many). The poet describes a cold, dawn farewell that foreshadows the relationship's tragic end, emphasizing themes of secrecy through imagery of hushed partings and private grief. The poet's bitterness is evident as they watch their former lover's name become tarnished in society, yet they still feel the sting of their shared past.

The poem powerfully conveys the lasting impact of a broken relationship, where the voice cannot find closure and experiences renewed pain upon hearing their former lover's name. Through its four stanzas, the poem masterfully depicts the universal experiences of regret, secret sorrow and the enduring nature of lost love.

When we two parted
　In silence and tears,
Half broken-hearted
　To sever for years,
Pale grew thy cheek and cold,
　Colder thy kiss;
Truly that hour foretold
　Sorrow to this.

The dew of the morning
　Sunk chill on my brow—
It felt like the warning
　Of what I feel now.
Thy vows are all broken,
　And light is thy fame;
I hear thy name spoken,
　And share in its shame.

They name thee before me,
　A knell to mine ear;
A shudder comes o'er me—
　Why wert thou so dear?
They know not I knew thee,
　Who knew thee too well—
Long, long shall I rue thee,
　Too deeply to tell.

In secret we met—
　In silence I grieve,

That thy heart could forget,
  Thy spirit deceive.
If I should meet thee
  After long years,
How should I greet thee?—
  With silence and tears.

CONDITION OR SITUATION:
The Pain of First Love

PRESCRIPTION:
First Love (1820)

by John Clare

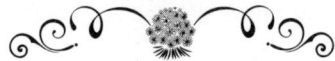

'First Love' is an intensely emotional poem that captures the overwhelming experience of falling in love for the first time. Clare describes the physical and psychological impact of seeing his first love, focusing on the dramatic bodily sensations and the complete transformation of his world in that moment.

The poem explores themes of love's intense physicality, with descriptions of the narrator's face turning pale, blood rushing, legs weakening and sight being altered. Clare portrays love as a force that literally stops the speaker in his tracks and permanently changes his perception of life. The imagery of winter turning to spring suggests the transformative power of love, while the closing stanzas reveal the pain of unrequited feelings.

The message conveys how first love is a profound, life-altering experience that can be both beautiful and painful. Clare shows that this initial encounter with love leaves an indelible mark on one's heart, creating both sweet memories and lasting wounds that can never be fully healed.

———————— ♦ ————————

I ne'er was struck before that hour
With love so sudden and so sweet,
Her face it bloomed like a sweet flower
And stole my heart away complete.
My face turned pale as deadly pale,
My legs refused to walk away,
And when she looked, 'what could I ail?'
My life and all seemed turned to clay.

And then my blood rushed to my face
And took my sight away,
The trees and bushes round the place
Seemed midnight at noonday.
I could not see a single thing,
Words from my eyes did start;
They spoke as chords do from the string
And blood burnt round my heart.

Are flowers the winter's choice?
Is love's bed always snow?

She seemed to hear my silent voice
And love's appeals to know.
I never saw so sweet a face
As that I stood before:
My heart has left its dwelling-place
And can return no more.

CONDITION OR SITUATION:
Age-Gap Relationships

PRESCRIPTION:
On Raglan Road (1946)
by Patrick Kavanagh

'On Raglan Road' is a deeply personal poem about unrequited love and the bittersweet nature of romantic passion. Kavanagh explores the experience of falling in love with a younger woman, knowing the relationship is likely doomed from the start. The poem is based on his real-life infatuation with Hilda Moriarty, a medical student.

The poem weaves together themes of love, regret and inevitable loss. Kavanagh uses natural imagery, particularly of autumn leaves, to symbolize the temporary nature of their connection. He acknowledges his own role in causing emotional pain by pursuing someone he knew was beyond his reach, comparing himself to a creature of the night courting the light of day.

The message centres on the inherent risks of love and how we sometimes willingly walk into emotional danger, despite knowing the likely outcome. It speaks to the universal experience of choosing to love even when we recognize it may lead to heartbreak.

On Raglan Road on an autumn day I met her first and knew
That her dark hair would weave a snare that I might one day rue;
I saw the danger, yet I walked along the enchanted way,
And I said, let grief be a fallen leaf at the dawning of the day.

On Grafton Street in November we tripped lightly along the ledge
Of the deep ravine where can be seen the worth of passion's pledge,
The Queen of Hearts still making tarts and I not making hay –
O I loved too much and by such and such is happiness thrown away.

I gave her gifts of the mind I gave her the secret sign that's known
To the artists who have known the true gods of sound and stone
And word and tint. I did not stint for I gave her poems to say.
With her own name there and her own dark hair like clouds over fields of May

On a quiet street where old ghosts meet I see her walking now
Away from me so hurriedly my reason must allow
That I had wooed not as I should a creature made of clay –
When the angel woos the clay he'd lose his wings at the dawn of day.

CONDITION OR SITUATION:
Love at First Sight

PRESCRIPTION:
Who Ever Loved That Loved Not at First Sight? (1598)

by Christopher Marlowe

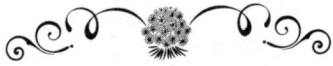

'Who Ever Loved That Loved Not at First Sight', by Christopher Marlowe from his epic poem, *Hero and Leander*, explores the powerful concept of love at first sight, drawing on classical mythology and Renaissance ideals of romantic love. The poem challenges readers to consider whether true love can exist without an immediate, instinctive attraction.

Through references to Hero and Leander's legendary romance and other mythological lovers, Marlowe argues that genuine love often strikes instantaneously. He presents love at first sight not as superficial attraction, but as a profound, almost divine connection that transcends rational thought and time.

The poem's themes interweave fate, desire and the immediacy of true love, suggesting that authentic romantic connections are predestined and recognizable in an instant. Marlowe's message emphasizes the overwhelming power of immediate attraction while elevating it beyond mere physical desire to something more spiritual and meaningful, reflecting Renaissance ideals about love's noble and transformative nature, presenting instant attraction as a sign of destiny.

It lies not in our power to love, or hate,
For will in us is over-rulde by fate.
When two are stript long ere the course begin,
We wish that one should lose, the other win.
And one especially doo we affect,
Of two gold Ingots like in each respect,
The reason no man knowes, let it suffise,
What we behold is censur'd by our eyes.
Where both deliberat, the love is slight,
Who ever lov'd, that lov'd not at first sight?

CONDITION OR SITUATION:
A Clandestine Love Affair

PRESCRIPTION:
Meeting at Night (1845)
by Robert Browning

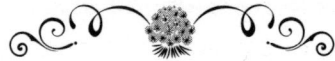

'Meeting at Night' is a passionate love poem that describes a secret romantic encounter, capturing both the physical journey and emotional intensity of clandestine love. Through rich sensory imagery and vivid descriptions of a nighttime coastal landscape, Browning traces the speaker's journey across sea and land to meet their lover.

The poem unfolds in two parts, first describing the journey across the dark waters and along the beach, then depicting the final moments of arrival and reunion. Browning employs evocative imagery of the sea, shore and farm landscape, creating a sense of urgency and anticipation. The progression from cold, grey seascape to warm, intimate interior reinforces the poem's movement from isolation to connection.

The central themes explore romantic passion, the thrill of forbidden love and the contrast between public and private worlds. The poem celebrates the intensity of romantic love and suggests that such powerful emotions make any journey or risk worthwhile.

The grey sea and the long black land;
And the yellow half-moon large and low;
And the startled little waves that leap
In fiery ringlets from their sleep,
As I gain the cove with pushing prow,
And quench its speed in the slushy sand.

Then a mile of warm sea-scented beach;
Three fields to cross till a farm appears;
A tap at the pane, the quick sharp scratch
And blue spurt of a lighted match,
And a voice less loud, thro' its joys and fears,
Than the two hearts beating each to each!

CONDITION OR SITUATION:
Girl Trouble

PRESCRIPTION:
Girlfriend (mid-20th century)

by Marina Tsvetaeva

'Girlfriend' by Marina Tsvetaeva is a powerful exploration of the complex emotions that exist between women. She portrays women as deeply connected while remaining acutely aware of their position as lovers, friends or potential romantic rivals. The poem examines the delicate balance between intimacy and competition, particularly in the context of romantic relationships and shared experiences.

Through direct and emotionally charged language, Tsvetaeva captures the paradoxical nature of female friendship. The poem reflects on the duality of these relationships and reveals how women can be both confidantes and competitors, sharing intimate secrets and moments while harbouring underlying jealousies. Composed in 1914, but published posthumously in 1941, it is the first in a cycle of poems which Tsvetaeva wrote to fellow Russian poet Sophia Parnok, with whom she had a passionate love affair.

Are you happy? You never tell me.
Maybe it's better like this.
You've kissed so many others –
which makes for sadness.
In you, I see the heroines
of Shakespeare's tragedies.
You, unhappy lady, were
never saved by anybody.
You have grown tired of repeating
the familiar words of love!
An iron ring on a bloodless hand
is more expressive,
I love you – like a storm-burst
overhead – I must confess it;
all the more fiercely because you burn

and bite, and most of all
because our secret lives take
very different paths:
seduction and dark fate
are your inspiration.
To you, my aquiline demon,
I apologise. In a flash –
as if over a coffin – I realise
it was always too late to save you!
Even as I tremble – it may be
I am dreaming – there
remains one enchanting irony:
for *you* – are not *he*.

CONDITION OR SITUATION:
Breaking Up with Someone

PRESCRIPTION:
Intimates (c.1932)

by D. H. Lawrence

The ultimate breakup poem, 'Intimates' by D. H. Lawrence explores the complex dynamics of a deteriorating relationship, focusing on the subtle hostilities and emotional distance between two people who were once close. The poem examines how intimacy can transform into a battlefield of antagonism, where familiar gestures become weapons and everyday interactions are laden with resentment.

The poem's tone conveys the bitter irony of 'intimates' who have become strangers while maintaining a façade of closeness. Through careful and caustic observation of small moments and gestures, Lawrence reveals how relationships can hollow out from within, leaving only a shell of former intimacy. The work ultimately comments on the painful paradox of knowing someone deeply while simultaneously growing apart from them.

Don't you care for my love? she said bitterly.

I handed her the mirror, and said:
Please address these questions to the proper person!
Please make all requests to head-quarters!
In all matters of emotional importance
please approach the supreme authority direct! -

So I handed her the mirror.
And she would have broken it over my head,
but she caught sight of her own reflection
and that held her spellbound for two seconds
while I fled.

CONDITION OR SITUATION:
Adultery

PRESCRIPTION:
The Faithless Wife (1928)

by Federico García Lorca

The thrill of adultery can have an intoxicating effect on people. 'The Faithless Wife' by Federico García Lorca explores themes of forbidden passion, betrayal and the consequences of illicit desire. The poem describes a passionate encounter between a narrator and a married woman who goes with him into the countryside. Through vivid sensory imagery and natural symbolism, García Lorca captures the intensity of their secret liaison and the moral complexity of adultery. The dark undertones of the poem suggest both the thrill and the guilt of forbidden love, with images of the night, darkness and distant lights representing the shadow world in which their affair exists.

The woman's infidelity is presented neither with judgement nor celebration, but rather as a fact of human desire and weakness. The poem's atmosphere is heavy with eroticism and danger, reflecting the Spanish cultural context of honour and shame. It examines how passion can override social conventions and moral obligations, leading to both pleasure and pain.

So I took her to the river
believing she was a maiden,
but she already had a husband.
It was on St. James night
and almost as if I was obliged to.
The lanterns went out
and the crickets lighted up.
In the farthest street corners
I touched her sleeping breasts
and they opened to me suddenly
like spikes of hyacinth.
The starch of her petticoat
sounded in my ears
like a piece of silk
rent by ten knives.
Without silver light on their foliage
the trees had grown larger
and a horizon of dogs
barked very far from the river.

Past the blackberries,
the reeds and the hawthorn
underneath her cluster of hair
I made a hollow in the earth
I took off my tie,
she took off her dress.
I, my belt with the revolver,
She, her four bodices.
Nor nard nor mother-o'-pearl
have skin so fine,

nor does glass with silver
shine with such brilliance.
Her thighs slipped away from me
like startled fish,
half full of fire,
half full of cold.
That night I ran
on the best of roads
mounted on a nacre mare
without bridle stirrups.

As a man, I won't repeat
the things she said to me.
The light of understanding
has made me more discreet.
Smeared with sand and kisses
I took her away from the river.
The swords of the lilies
battled with the air.

I behaved like what I am,
like a proper gypsy.
I gave her a large sewing basket,
of straw-coloured satin,
but I did not fall in love
for although she had a husband
she told me she was a maiden
when I took her to the river.

CONDITION OR SITUATION:
Pain of Separation

PRESCRIPTION:
A Red, Red Rose (1794)
by Robert Burns

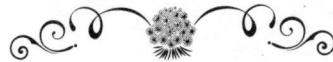

'A Red, Red Rose' by Scottish poet Robert Burns is one of the most enduring love lyrics in the English language. Burns was a pioneer of the Romantic Movement, and this poem demonstrates key Romantic themes such as the celebration of nature, emotion and local tradition.

Written in 1794, the poem's simple lyrics add a powerful sincerity and tenderness to the speaker's declaration. Its regular rhythm and refrain-like repetition mirror the cadence of traditional Scots song, which, alongside the use of the Scots dialect, adds a somewhat carefree, everyday quality to this weighty vow of devotion.

Beneath its simplicity lies a profound faith in love's endurance against time and distance – even 'Till a' the seas gang dry, my dear, And the rocks melt w' the sun:' and the lovers are separated by 'ten thousand mile', the speaker will remain devoted to their lover.

O, my luve's like a red, red rose,
   That's newly sprung in June:
O, my luve's like the melodie
   That's sweetly play'd in tune.

As fair art thou, my bonnie lass,
   So deep in luve am I;
And I will luve thee still, my dear,
   Till a' the seas gang dry.

Till a' the seas gang dry, my dear,
   And the rocks melt w' the sun:
I will luve thee still, my dear,
   While the sands o' life shall run.

And fare thee weel, my only luve!
   And fare thee weel a while!
And I will come again, my luve,
   Tho' it were ten thousand mile.

CONDITION OR SITUATION:
Appreciating Quality Time with a Loved One

PRESCRIPTION:
An Hour with Thee (c.1826)
by Walter Scott

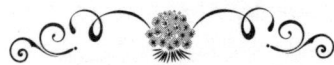

'An Hour with Thee' by Sir Walter Scott is a romantic lyric poem that celebrates the profound value of brief moments spent with a loved one. The poem emphasizes how a single hour in the presence of the beloved is worth more than any worldly pleasures or material wealth. Through passionate declarations, Scott illustrates how time becomes more precious when spent with someone cherished, suggesting that such moments contain more true life and meaning than years spent apart.

Scott presents a treatise on the intensity of romantic love and its ability to transform ordinary time into something extraordinary. The poem ultimately conveys that love's quality transcends quantity, making even the briefest encounter with the beloved more valuable than a lifetime of other experiences.

An hour with thee! When earliest day
Dapples with gold the eastern grey,
Oh, what can frame my mind to bear

The toil and turmoil, cark and care,
New griefs, which coming hours unfold,
And sad remembrance of the old?
One hour with thee.

One hour with thee! When burning June
Waves his red flag at pitch of noon;
What shall repay the faithful swain,
His labour on the sultry plain;
And, more than cave or sheltering bough,
Cool feverish blood and throbbing brow?
One hour with thee.

One hour with thee! When sun is set,
Oh, what can teach me to forget
The thankless labours of the day;
The hopes, the wishes, flung away;
The increasing wants, and lessening gains,
The master's pride, who scorns my pains?
One hour with thee.

CONDITION OR SITUATION:
Falling in Love Late in Life

PRESCRIPTION:
The Last Love (c.1854)

by Fyodor Tyutchev

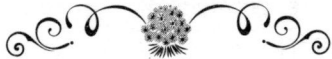

While finding love late in life can be a cause of great comfort and joy for some people, especially for those who may have abandoned any thought of ever loving again, 'The Last Love' by Fyodor Tyutchev portrays it as a bittersweet experience – one that is both a blessing and a poignant reminder of our mortality.

The poet uses natural imagery, particularly the metaphor of autumn's fading light, to convey how this final love glows more brightly against the approaching darkness of life's end. The poem's central message emphasizes how love can rejuvenate the spirit even as the body ages, while acknowledging the melancholy of a passion that comes too late. The poem ultimately celebrates the power of love to illuminate life's twilight while accepting its temporal nature.

Oh, how, in the ending years
Is love more tender and superstitious –
O shine! O shine, my parting rays
Of the evening sun, of the last heart wishes!

The darkness cuts half of the sky;
And only the West has the roving glow,
Oh, time of evening, do not fly!
Enchantment, be prolonged and slow!

Let blood in veins has a thinner staff,
But a heart preserves the gentle passion –
O you, my last and tender love,
You are my bliss and desperation.

CONDITION OR SITUATION:

Beguiled by the Nature of True Love

PRESCRIPTION:

The Definition of Love (1681)

by Andrew Marvell

In his poem 'The Definition of Love', Andrew Marvell sets out to 'do what it says on the tin' as he explores the paradoxical nature of perfect love and its relationship to fate and impossibility. He describes love as something that exists in its purest form when it is not physically realized. Confused by this paradox? Read on.

The poem suggests that the lovers' devotion is so perfect that fate itself conspires to keep them apart, as their union would threaten the very order of the universe. Using complex metaphysical conceits, Marvell presents love as parallel lines that can never meet, despite their perfect alignment. He argues that the most sublime form of love is one that remains unconsummated, existing in an ideal spiritual realm rather than the physical world.

The poet ultimately presents a sophisticated philosophical argument about the nature of perfect love, suggesting that its very perfection makes its earthly fulfilment impossible. Put that in your metaphysical pipe and smoke it!

My Love is of a birth as rare
As 'tis for object strange and high:
It was begotten by despair
Upon Impossibility.

Magnanimous Despair alone
Could show me so divine a thing,
Where feeble Hope could ne'r have flown
But vainly flapt its Tinsel Wing.

And yet I quickly might arrive
Where my extended Soul is fixt,
But Fate does Iron wedges drive,
And always crowds it self betwixt.

For Fate with jealous Eye does see
Two perfect Loves; nor lets them close:
Their union would her ruine be,
And her Tyrannick pow'er depose.

And therefore her Decreees of Steel
Us as the distant Poles have plac'd,
(Though Love's whole World on us doth wheel)
Not by themselves to be embrac'd.

Unless the giddy Heaven fall,
And Earth some new Convulsion tear;
And, us to join, the World should all
Be cramp'd into a Planisphere.

As Lines, so Loves oblique may well
Themselves in every Angle greet:
But ours so truly Parallel,
Though infinite can never meet.

Therefore the Love which us doth bind,
But Fate so enviously debarrs,
Is the Conjunction of the Mind,
And Opposition of the Stars.

CONDITION OR SITUATION:
Missed Opportunities in Love

PRESCRIPTION:
You Would Have Understood Me, Had You Waited (1896)
by Ernest Dowson

The poem 'You Would Have Understood Me, Had You Waited' is a curiosity in that it is thought to be a translation of a poem by Paul Verlaine, but it has been so immaculately rendered into English and radically altered by the Victorian poet Ernest Dowson that really it is Dowson's poem, inspired by Paul Verlaine.

The poem explores the themes of longing, regret and the pain of missed opportunities in love. The speaker reflects on a relationship that could have blossomed into true love if only patience and faith had prevailed. Dowson's delicate, melancholic tone reveals the sorrow of love lost not through hostility, but through timing and misunderstanding. The central message conveys how fragile and fleeting love can be, and how easily it can slip away if not nurtured with trust and perseverance. Ultimately, the poem laments what might have been, evoking a sense of wistfulness and emphasizing the lasting ache of unrealized affection.

You would have understood me, had you waited;
   I could have loved you, dear! as well as he:
Had we not been impatient, dear! and fated
      Always to disagree.

What is the use of speech? Silence were fitter:
   Lest we should still be wishing things unsaid.
Though all the words we ever spake were bitter,
      Shall I reproach you dead?

Nay, let this earth, your portion, likewise cover
   All the old anger, setting us apart:
Always, in all, in truth was I your lover;
      Always, I held your heart.

I have met other women who were tender,
   As you were cold, dear! with a grace as rare.
Think you, I turned to them, or made surrender,
      I who had found you fair?

Had we been patient, dear! ah, had you waited,
   I had fought death for you, better than he:
But from the very first, dear! we were fated
      Always to disagree.

Late, late, I come to you, now death discloses
   Love that in life was not to be our part:
On your low lying mound between the roses,
      Sadly I cast my heart.

I would not waken you: nay! this is fitter;
   Death and the darkness give you unto me;
Here we who loved so, were so cold and bitter,
       Hardly can disagree.

CONDITION OR SITUATION:
Getting Over It

PRESCRIPTION:
Between Us Now (1912)

by Thomas Hardy

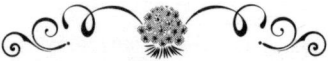

'Between Us Now' by Thomas Hardy poignantly explores the themes of lost love, emotional disconnection and the irreversible nature of time. The poem captures the bittersweet reality of how relationships can dissolve despite having once meant so much. Through its melancholic tone, Hardy illustrates how time creates an insurmountable distance between former lovers, turning passionate connections into mere memories.

The poet grapples with both regret for what was lost and resignation to the fact that the past cannot be changed. The poem highlights how time inevitably transforms relationships, leaving individuals to confront the gap between their past hopes and present reality. It serves as a meditation on the impermanence of human connections and the lasting impact of love long after it has ended.

Between us now and here —
   Two thrown together
Who are not wont to wear
   Life's flushest feather —
Who see the scenes slide past,
The daytimes dimming fast,
Let there be truth at last,
   Even if despair.

So thoroughly and long
   Have you now known me,
So real in faith and strong
   Have I now shown me,
That nothing needs disguise
Further in any wise,
Or asks or justifies
   A guarded tongue.

Face unto face, then, say,
   Eyes mine own meeting,
Is your heart far away,
   Or with mine beating?
When false things are brought low,
And swift things have grown slow,
Feigning like froth shall go,
   Faith be for aye.

CONDITION OR SITUATION:
The Pain of Being a Jilted Lover

PRESCRIPTION:
Farewell Ungrateful Traitor (1681)

by John Dryden

It's not much fun being unceremoniously dumped, but John Dryden finds some solace in the bitterness of being jilted by a lover. 'Farewell Ungrateful Traitor' explores themes of betrayal, pride and emotional liberation following the end of a deceptive relationship. The poem's speaker addresses those who have been disloyal and unappreciative, expressing both pain at their treachery and a sense of triumph in breaking free from their influence. Dryden emphasizes the value of self-respect and the necessity of releasing attachments to those who do not reciprocate loyalty or affection.

The poem ultimately delivers a message of personal empowerment, encouraging the reader to find strength in moving on and to appreciate the freedom gained after distancing oneself from toxic alliances. Through its resolute tone, the poem suggests that emotional honesty and personal dignity are more important than clinging to false relationships.

Farewell, ungrateful traitor!
  Farewell, my perjured swain!
Let never injured creature
  Believe a man again.
The pleasure of possessing
Surpasses all expressing,
But 'tis too short a blessing,
  And love too long a pain.

'Tis easy to deceive us,
  In pity of your pain;
But when we love, you leave us,
  To rail at you in vain.
Before we have descried it,
There is no bless beside it;
But she that once has tried it,
  Will never love again.

The passion you pretended
  Was only to obtain;
But when the charm is ended,
  The charmer you disdain.
Your love by ours we measure,
Till we have lost our treasure;
But dying is a pleasure,
  When living is a pain.

CONDITION OR SITUATION:
Head over Heels in Love

PRESCRIPTION:
Renouncement (1893)

by Alice Meynell

To be so giddy in love is a bittersweet experience, particularly, as Alice Meynell describes, if the object of your affection fills your every waking thought, no matter how hard you try to distract yourself.

Meynell's sonnet 'Renouncement' describes the poet's attempt to shun all thoughts of her beloved, perhaps because they are unattainable or their consummation illicit in the eyes of others. Meynell wrote during the Victorian era when female sexuality was severely repressed by societal constraints and convention, and the poem in one sense can be read as indicative of this repression, which 'must never, never come in sight'. Thankfully, we can all escape to our dreams, as the poet acknowledges at the end of the poem.

I must not think of thee; and, tired yet strong,
   I shun the thought that lurks in all delight—
   The thought of thee—and in the blue Heaven's height,
And in the sweetest passage of a song.

Oh, just beyond the fairest thoughts that throng
   This breast, the thought of thee waits, hidden yet bright;
   But it must never, never come in sight;
I must stop short of thee the whole day long.

But when sleep comes to close each difficult day,
   When night gives pause to the long watch I keep,
   And all my bonds I needs must loose apart,

Must doff my will as raiment laid away,—
   With the first dream that comes with the first sleep
   I run, I run, I am gather'd to thy heart.

2

Remedies for the Soul and Spirit

CONDITION OR SITUATION:
Learning to Cope with Loss

PRESCRIPTION:
One Art (1976)

by Elizabeth Bishop

Taken from her 1976 collection *Geography III*, 'One Art' by American poet Elizabeth Bishop is an example of a villanelle, a nineteen-line poem consisting of stanzas of five tercets (three lines) and a closing quatrain (four lines). The villanelle form evolved from folk ballads and peasant songs, and traditionally it had pastoral themes.

'One Art' is unusual in that it has a confessional voice (Bishop often professed a distaste for confessional poetry) with two alternating rhetorical refrains as the poet lists things she has 'lost' throughout her life. She tries to convince herself that their loss is just part of life and that she will prevail in spite of their absence. In the last stanza, however, the tone shifts to one of sombre acceptance of the deep grief of losing a loved one.

The art of losing isn't hard to master;
so many things seem filled with the intent
to be lost that their loss is no disaster.

Lose something every day. Accept the fluster
of lost door keys, the hour badly spent.
The art of losing isn't hard to master.

Then practice losing farther, losing faster:
places, and names, and where it was you meant
to travel. None of these will bring disaster.

I lost my mother's watch. And look! my last, or
next-to-last, of three loved houses went.
The art of losing isn't hard to master.

I lost two cities, lovely ones. And, vaster,
some realms I owned, two rivers, a continent.
I miss them, but it wasn't a disaster.

—Even losing you (the joking voice, a gesture
I love) I shan't have lied. It's evident
the art of losing's not too hard to master
though it may look like (*Write* it!) a disaster.

CONDITION OR SITUATION:
Grief and Mourning

PRESCRIPTION:
Remember (1849)

by Christina Rossetti

Dealing with the imminent death of a loved one is daunting and every day seems like a step toward the unknown, or as Shakespeare's Hamlet adroitly described it, 'the undiscovered country' (in this case 'the silent land'). This classic Victorian sonnet explores impending grief and is told from the point of view, not of the mourner, but of the person to be mourned.

The poem begins with a strong request to remember the protagonist, emphasizing the deep love and connection between them and their lover. The speaker acknowledges the possibility of forgetting and declares that they don't wish their beloved to feel burdened by guilt if they move on. Their final wish is that their beloved find joy and contentment, even if it means forgetting them.

Remember me when I am gone away,
   Gone far away into the silent land;
   When you can no more hold me by the hand,
Nor I half turn to go yet turning stay.
Remember me when no more day by day

You tell me of our future that you plann'd:
　Only remember me; you understand
It will be late to counsel then or pray.
Yet if you should forget me for a while
　And afterwards remember, do not grieve:
　For if the darkness and corruption leave
　A vestige of the thoughts that once I had,
Better by far you should forget and smile
　Than that you should remember and be sad.

CONDITION OR SITUATION:
In Need of Spiritual Sustenance

PRESCRIPTION:
Beauty Is a Waving Tree (14th century)
by Hafiz

'Beauty Is a Waving Tree' was composed by the great Persian poet Hafiz in the fourteenth century and translated into English by Elizabeth Daryush in 1921. It is a poem that conveys a profound spiritual message about the nature of beauty and divine love.

The central theme is that beauty, particularly in nature (symbolized by the waving tree), is a manifestation of divine presence and the grace of God. Hafiz proposes that when we truly see and appreciate beauty in its natural form, we are actually witnessing God's expression in the world. The poem emphasizes that beauty is not just a surface-level aesthetic experience, but rather a deeper, spiritual connection that can help us understand and feel closer to the divine.

Beauty is a waving tree,
    Beauty is a flower,
Beauty is a grassy lea
    & a shady bower,
Beauty is the verdant Spring
In our hearts awakening.

Beauty is a summer sun
    Warming all the land,
Whose full bounty doth o'errun
    More than our demand;
Spreadeth Beauty her kind feast
Lavishly for man & beast.

Autumn's quiet hast thou too,
    Beauty, who canst feed
Every craving, known or new
    Of the spirit's need,
Laying up a lasting store
Of ripe bliss for evermore.

O true Beauty, though joy's vain
    Seasons come & go,
Thou a refuge dost remain
    From all wintry woe,
Thou art still the perfect clime
Where no transience is nor time.

CONDITION OR SITUATION:
Struggling with Grief

PRESCRIPTION:
Futility (1918)

by Wilfred Owen

'Futility' by Wilfred Owen is a tender and sorrowful lament, mourning the death of an unknown soldier on the battlefield, probably in the snow, during World War 1. The poem was written in 1918, just a few months before Owen himself died in action in France on 4 November (one week before the end of the war).

'Futility' differs from Owen's earlier poems, which addressed the horrors of war far more graphically. With its quiet, poignant tone, it focuses on personal loss and the meaningless waste of life. Yet the poem also goes further, reflecting on the very nature of existence: 'O what made fatuous sunbeams toil / To break earth's sleep at all?' and leaving the reader in deep contemplation of the fragility of life.

Move him into the sun—
Gently its touch awoke him once,
At home, whispering of fields unsown.
Always it woke him, even in France,
Until this morning and this snow.
If anything might rouse him now
The kind old sun will know.

Think how it wakes the seeds—
Woke once the clays of a cold star.
Are limbs, so dear-achieved, are sides
Full-nerved, still warm, too hard to stir?
Was it for this the clay grew tall?
—O what made fatuous sunbeams toil
To break earth's sleep at all?

CONDITION OR SITUATION:
When Triumph Is Tempered by Grief

PRESCRIPTION:
O Captain! My Captain! (1865)

by Walt Whitman

Five days after the Confederate Army surrendered to the Unionists, President Abraham Lincoln was assassinated. 'O Captain! My Captain!' is Walt Whitman's emotional tribute to him. The poem uses an extended metaphor, portraying Lincoln as the captain of a ship (representing the United States) that has successfully completed its difficult voyage (the Civil War) but at a terrible cost.

The central message is that even in moments of great achievement and celebration, we must acknowledge the sacrifices made to reach them. The poem captures the bittersweet nature of the Union's victory and the profound sense of loss associated with Lincoln's death. The poem's popularity was revived in the twentieth century after the assassination of President John F. Kennedy, and it was later immortalized in the 1989 film, *Dead Poets Society*.

O Captain! my Captain! our fearful trip is done,
The ship has weather'd every rack, the prize we sought is won,
The port is near, the bells I hear, the people all exulting,
While follow eyes the steady keel, the vessel grim and daring;
    But O heart! heart! heart!
      O the bleeding drops of red,
        Where on the deck my Captain lies,
          Fallen cold and dead.

O Captain! my Captain! rise up and hear the bells;
Rise up – for you the flag is flung – for you the bugle trills,
For you bouquets and ribbon'd wreaths – for you the shores a-crowding,
For you they call, the swaying mass, their eager faces turning;
    Here Captain! dear father!
      This arm beneath your head!
        It is some dream that on the deck,
          You've fallen cold and dead.

My Captain does not answer, his lips are pale and still,
My father does not feel my arm, he has no pulse nor will,
The ship is anchor'd safe and sound, its voyage closed and done,
From fearful trip the victor ship comes in with object won;
    Exult O shores, and ring O bells!
      But I with mournful tread,
        Walk the deck my Captain lies,
          Fallen cold and dead.

CONDITION OR SITUATION:
Contemplating Mortality

PRESCRIPTION:
Do Not Go Gentle into That Good Night (1951)
by Dylan Thomas

'Do Not Go Gentle into That Good Night' is Dylan Thomas' passionate plea to his dying father, exploring themes of mortality, resistance against death and the fierce desire to hold on to life. The poem uses the villanelle form to emphasize its central message that death should be confronted with defiance rather than quiet acceptance. Thomas examines different types of men – wise, good, wild and grave – all unified in their rage against mortality. The recurring refrain urges resistance against death's darkness, suggesting that even at life's end, one should burn with passion and vitality.

The personal nature of the poem becomes clear in the final stanza, where Thomas directly addresses his father, begging him to fight against approaching death with fierce emotion. The overall message champions the human spirit's resistance to inevitable mortality, suggesting that life should be relinquished only after an impassioned struggle, not with passive resignation.

Do not go gentle into that good night,
Old age should burn and rave at close of day;
Rage, rage against the dying of the light.

Though wise men at their end know dark is right,
Because their words had forked no lightning they
Do not go gentle into that good night.

Good men, the last wave by, crying how bright
Their frail deeds might have danced in a green bay,
Rage, rage against the dying of the light.

Wild men who caught and sang the sun in flight,
And learn, too late, they grieved it on its way,
Do not go gentle into that good night.

Grave men, near death, who see with blinding sight
Blind eyes could blaze like meteors and be gay,
Rage, rage against the dying of the light.

And you, my father, there on the sad height,
Curse, bless, me now with your fierce tears, I pray.
Do not go gentle into that good night.
Rage, rage against the dying of the light.

CONDITION OR SITUATION:
Bereavement

PRESCRIPTION:
Funeral Blues (1938)
by W. H. Auden

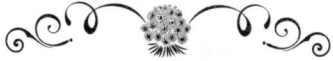

'Funeral Blues' by W. H. Auden explores the overwhelming nature of grief and the way profound loss can make the world seem meaningless to those left behind. The poem progresses from public displays of mourning to deeply personal expressions of despair, showing how the death of a loved one affects both the social and intimate spheres of life.

Auden illustrates how loss can make everyday elements of life seem pointless, from the mundane (airplanes, doves, traffic) to the cosmic (stars, moon, sun). The speaker's pain is so consuming that they wish to dismantle the entire universe, reflecting how personal grief can feel like the end of all meaning. The poem conveys the message that true love makes the beloved integral to one's existence, and their death creates a void that seems to negate all purpose and joy in life. Through powerful imagery and increasing emotional intensity, Auden captures the all-consuming nature of bereavement.

Stop all the clocks, cut off the telephone,
Prevent the dog from barking with a juicy bone,

Silence the pianos and with muffled drum
Bring out the coffin, let the mourners come.

Let aeroplanes circle moaning overhead
Scribbling on the sky the message 'He is Dead'.
Put crepe bows round the white necks of the public doves,
Let the traffic policemen wear black cotton gloves.

He was my North, my South, my East and West,
My working week and my Sunday rest,
My noon, my midnight, my talk, my song;
I thought that love would last forever: I was wrong.

The stars are not wanted now; put out every one,
Pack up the moon and dismantle the sun,
Pour away the ocean and sweep up the wood;
For nothing now can ever come to any good.

CONDITION OR SITUATION:
When All Seems Lost

PRESCRIPTION:
Hope Is the Thing with Feathers (1891)

by Emily Dickinson

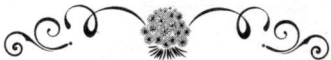

Emily Dickinson's 'Hope Is the Thing with Feathers' is a powerful poem that personifies hope as a resilient bird perching in the soul. Through this metaphor, she explores the unshakeable nature of hope, depicting it as a constant presence, singing its tune without words. The poem emphasizes hope's persistence through life's hardest moments, symbolized by the 'storm' and 'gale', suggesting hope's ability to sustain us through our darkest times. The bird's song, though wordless, provides warmth and comfort in the 'chillest land' and on the 'strangest sea', a universal presence across all human experiences.

The final stanza reveals hope's selfless nature, noting that it never asks for anything, not even 'a crumb', yet continues to give strength and inspiration, portraying hope as a pure, unconditional force that sustains human resilience.

Hope is the thing with feathers
That perches in the soul,

And sings the tune without the words,
And never stops at all,

And sweetest in the gale is heard;
And sore must be the storm
That could abash the little bird
That kept so many warm.

I've heard it in the chillest land,
And on the strangest sea;
Yet, never, in extremity,
It asked a crumb of me.

CONDITION OR SITUATION:
In Need of Strength and Resilience

PRESCRIPTION:
Lines Composed in a Wood on a Windy Day (1842)
by Anne Brontë

'Lines Composed in a Wood on a Windy Day' by Anne Brontë is a contemplative poem that explores the relationship between nature, human emotion and spiritual resilience. Through vivid descriptions of wind moving through trees, the youngest of the Brontë sisters creates a parallel between nature's strength and human perseverance through difficult times.

In the poem, the speaker finds solace and inspiration in watching trees bend but not break under the pressure of strong winds, using this as a metaphor for human endurance during life's challenges. The wind represents life's trials, while the trees symbolize the human spirit's capacity to remain steadfast.

Brontë's message emphasizes that, like trees bending and swaying but maintaining their roots, humans can remain strong while facing adversity. The poem suggests that there is beauty and strength in flexibility, and that nature serves as a model for human resilience.

My soul is awakened, my spirit is soaring
And carried aloft on the wings of the breeze;
For above and around me the wild wind is roaring,
Arousing to rapture the earth and the seas.

The long withered grass in the sunshine is glancing,
The bare trees are tossing their branches on high;
The dead leaves beneath them are merrily dancing,
The white clouds are scudding across the blue sky.

I wish I could see how the ocean is lashing
The foam of its billows to whirlwinds of spray;
I wish I could see how its proud waves are dashing,
And hear the wild roar of their thunder today!

CONDITION OR SITUATION:
In Need of a Divine Epiphany

PRESCRIPTION:
The Windhover (1918)

by Gerard Manley Hopkins

'The Windhover' by Gerard Manley Hopkins is a masterful sonnet dedicated 'to Christ Our Lord' that celebrates the majestic flight of a falcon as a symbol of divine beauty and spiritual revelation. Through Hopkins' distinctive sprung rhythm (a metric form that counts accents in a line instead of syllables) and rich language, the poem captures a moment of transcendent wonder as the speaker observes the bird's graceful mastery of the wind.

The poem transforms the falcon's ordinary morning flight into an extraordinary display of natural glory, suggesting that within this simple act lies evidence of divine presence. Hopkins uses vivid imagery and compound words to convey the bird's dynamic movements, comparing its beauty to the mastery of a knight-at-arms and the danger of a drawn sword.

The poem's deeper message reveals how moments of natural beauty can lead to spiritual enlightenment, with the bird's physical grace pointing toward Christ's sacrifice and glory. Through this observation of natural splendour, Hopkins suggests that divine beauty can be found in everyday moments, connecting earthly and heavenly realms.

I caught this morning morning's minion, king-
    dom of daylight's dauphin, dapple-dawn-drawn Falcon, in
        his riding
  Of the rolling level underneath him steady air, and striding
High there, how he rung upon the rein of a wimpling wing
In his ecstasy! then off, off forth on swing,
    As a skate's heel sweeps smooth on a bow-bend: the hurl
        and gliding
  Rebuffed the big wind. My heart in hiding
Stirred for a bird,—the achieve of; the mastery of the thing!

Brute beauty and valour and act, oh, air, pride, plume, here
    Buckle! AND the fire that breaks from thee then, a billion
Times told lovelier, more dangerous, O my chevalier!

    No wonder of it: shéer plód makes plough down sillion
Shine, and blue-bleak embers, ah my dear,
Fall, gall themselves, and gash gold-vermillion.

CONDITION OR SITUATION:
Searching for Inner Strength

PRESCRIPTION:
The Sentence (1989)

by Anna Akhmatova

'The Sentence' by Anna Akhmatova is part of a cycle of poems titled *Requiem* that forms a powerful reflection on personal and collective suffering during Stalin's Great Terror in Soviet Russia. It was written after her son was arrested and subsequently sentenced to five years in a Siberian *Gulag* (forced labour camp).

The poem portrays themes of maternal love, political oppression and human resilience in the face of totalitarian brutality. Akhmatova's use of stark imagery and emotional restraint emphasizes the quiet dignity of her grief. The 'sentence' of the title refers not only to the prison terms, but also to the metaphorical sentence these women must serve waiting for news of loved ones. The work serves as both a personal lamentation and a historical document, giving voice to the silent suffering of countless families torn apart by political repression.

And the stone word fell
On my still-living breast.

Never mind, I was ready.
I will manage somehow.

Today I have so much to do:
I must kill memory once and for all,
I must turn my soul to stone,
I must learn to live again—

Unless ... Summer's ardent rustling
Is like a festival outside my window.
For a long time I've foreseen this
Brilliant day, deserted house.

CONDITION OR SITUATION:
Contemplating Mortality

PRESCRIPTION:
All the World's a Stage (1623)

by William Shakespeare

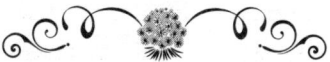

'All the World's a Stage' from *As You Like It* by William Shakespeare is a contemplative exploration of mortality and the transitory nature of human existence. Through the extended metaphor of life as a theatrical performance,

Shakespeare divides human life into seven roles – from infancy to old age. The final stage presents death as a gradual return to nothingness. This device strips death of drama, showing it as the quiet, inevitable finale to life's performance – the natural conclusion of a predetermined script.

It is a philosophical piece that encourages reflection rather than fear, urging us to recognize life as a series of passing roles, each contributing to the whole before we make our exit.

All the world's a stage,
And all the men and women merely players;
They have their exits and their entrances;
And one man in his time plays many parts,
His acts being seven ages. At first the infant,
Mewling and puking in the nurse's arms;
And then the whining school-boy, with his satchel
And shining morning face, creeping like snail
Unwillingly to school. And then the lover,
Sighing like furnace, with a woeful ballad
Made to his mistress' eyebrow. Then a soldier,
Full of strange oaths, and bearded like the pard,
Jealous in honour, sudden and quick in quarrel,
Seeking the bubble reputation
Even in the cannon's mouth. And then the justice,
In fair round belly with good capon lin'd,
With eyes severe and beard of formal cut,
Full of wise saws and modern instances;
And so he plays his part. The sixth age shifts
Into the lean and slipper'd pantaloon,

With spectacles on nose and pouch on side;
His youthful hose, well sav'd, a world too wide
For his shrunk shank; and his big manly voice,
Turning again toward childish treble, pipes
And whistles in his sound. Last scene of all,
That ends this strange eventful history,
Is second childishness and mere oblivion;
Sans teeth, sans eyes, sans taste, sans everything.

CONDITION OR SITUATION:
Existential Despair

PRESCRIPTION:
The Hollow Men
(Stanzas I and V) (1925)

by T. S. Eliot

'The Hollow Men' by T. S. Eliot delves into themes of spiritual emptiness, paralysis and existential despair in the aftermath of the First World War. The opening stanza of the poem introduces a world characterized by fragmentation and disconnection, where individuals with desolate inner landscapes are stripped of purpose and unable to take meaningful action. Haunted by guilt, regret and a distant sense of loss, these 'hollow men' are emotionally and morally vacant.

The poem goes on to question the possibility of redemption, and highlights the difficulty of achieving genuine expression or transformation. Its haunting conclusion emphasizes the anticlimactic and uncertain end of both lives and civilizations, encapsulated in the famous lines, 'This is the way the world ends / Not with a bang but a whimper.' Ultimately, Eliot's message is a sombre reflection on the human condition in a disjointed, spiritually barren world.

I

We are the hollow men
We are the stuffed men
Leaning together
Headpiece filled with straw. Alas!
Our dried voices, when
We whisper together
Are quiet and meaningless
As wind in dry grass
Or rats' feet over broken glass
In our dry cellar

Shape without form, shade without colour,
Paralysed force, gesture without motion;

Those who have crossed
With direct eyes, to death's other Kingdom

Remember us – if at all – not as lost
Violent souls, but only
As the hollow men
The stuffed men.

V

Here we go round the prickly pear
Prickly pear prickly pear
Here we go round the prickly pear
At five o'clock in the morning.
Between the idea
And the reality
Between the motion
And the act
Falls the Shadow
    For Thine is the Kingdom
Between the conception
And the creation
Between the emotion
And the response
Falls the Shadow
    Life is very long
Between the desire
And the spasm
Between the potency
And the existence
Between the essence
And the descent
Falls the Shadow
    For Thine is the Kingdom

For Thine is
Life is
For Thine is the
This is the way the world ends
This is the way the world ends
This is the way the world ends
Not with a bang but a whimper.

CONDITION OR SITUATION:
Grappling with Despair

PRESCRIPTION:
In a Dark Time (1960)

by Theodore Roethke

Dr Samuel Johnson referred to his frequent bouts of depression as 'visitations from The Black Dog'. Theodore Roethke, conversely, seems to almost relish entertaining obscure, dark canines in his poem 'In a Dark Time'.

The poem delves into the psychological descent that accompanies personal crisis, describing the intense confusion and chaos experienced during times of darkness. As Roethke journeys through this turmoil, he confronts his fears and vulnerabilities, ultimately recognizing that facing darkness is essential for self-understanding. Through vivid natural imagery and paradoxical statements, the poem suggests that madness and clarity, light and shadow, are intertwined aspects of the human experience.

The process of grappling with despair leads to profound insight, revealing the strength found within suffering. Overall, Roethke's message is that enduring and embracing one's darkest moments can often lead to greater wisdom and a deeper connection to the self, affirming that this darkness is not an end but a necessary passage in the journey toward self-realization.

In a dark time, the eye begins to see,
I meet my shadow in the deepening shade;
I hear my echo in the echoing wood—
A lord of nature weeping to a tree.
I live between the heron and the wren,
Beasts of the hill and serpents of the den.
What's madness but nobility of soul
At odds with circumstance? The day's on fire!
I know the purity of pure despair,
My shadow pinned against a sweating wall.
That place among the rocks—is it a cave,
Or a winding path? The edge is what I have.

A steady storm of correspondences!
A night flowing with birds, a ragged moon,
And in broad day the midnight come again!
A man goes far to find out what he is—

Death of the self in a long, tearless night,
All natural shapes blazing unnatural light.

Dark, dark my light, and darker my desire.
My soul, like some heat-maddened summer fly,
Keeps buzzing at the sill. Which I is *I*?
A fallen man, I climb out of my fear.
The mind enters itself, and God the mind,
And one is One, free in the tearing wind.

CONDITION OR SITUATION:
Wishing Upon a Star

PRESCRIPTION:
Stars (1926)

by Sara Teasdale

'Stars' by Sara Teasdale explores themes of solitude, longing and the search for connection amid isolation. The poem captures the poet's awareness of the beauty and constancy of the stars, which serve as silent witnesses to her inner world. While she finds comfort in their distant, enduring presence, she also expresses a deep yearning for human understanding and companionship. The stars symbolize both the solace of something eternal and the painful reminder of her loneliness.

Teasdale's message centres on the experience of solace and sadness that arises from contemplating the vast universe and one's place within it. Through this reflection, the poem gently suggests that while we may find peace in nature's everlasting patterns, the human need for closeness and empathy remains powerful, shaping our emotional landscape even in the quiet darkness beneath the stars.

Alone in the night
On a dark hill
With pines around me
Spicy and still,

And a heaven full of stars
Over my head
White and topaz
And misty red;

Myriads with beating
Hearts of fire
The aeons
Cannot vex or tire;

Up the dome of heaven
Like a great hill
I watch them marching
Stately and still.

And I know that I
Am honored to be
Witness
Of so much majesty.

CONDITION OR SITUATION:
Struggling to Say Farewell

PRESCRIPTION:
Good-bye (1921)
by Walter de la Mare

Bidding a loved one goodbye can be hard words to say: 'The last of all last words spoken' as portrayed in Walter de la Mare's poignant poem 'Good-bye'. The poem illustrates the bitter emotions that arise when we let go, highlighting both the sadness of departure and lingering memories of heartbreak. He captures the weight of those last words as the present falls away into the darkness of loss and uses delicate imagery to evoke the poignancy of final departure. Both a plucked flower and the solitary sound of a distant bell highlight a sense of approaching emptiness. 'Good-bye' is a moving meditation on loss and the transitory nature of existence.

The last of last words spoken is, Good-bye –
The last dismantled flower in the weed-grown hedge,
The last thin rumour of a feeble bell far ringing,
The last blind rat to spurn the mildewed rye.

A hardening darkness glasses the haunted eye,
Shines into nothing the watcher's burnt-out candle,
Wreathes into scentless nothing the wasting incense,
Faints in the outer silence the hunting-cry.

Love of its muted music breathes no sigh,
Thought in her ivory tower gropes in her spinning,
Toss on in vain the whispering trees of Eden,
Last of all last words spoken is, Good-bye.

CONDITION OR SITUATION:
Beset by Earthly Worries

PRESCRIPTION:
The Jackdaw (1782)

by William Cowper

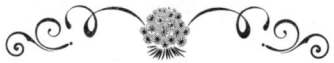

One of the elements of stoic philosophy when beset by earthly worries, those everyday concerns that weigh so heavy on heart and mind, is to try to take 'the view from above'. 'The Jackdaw' by William Cowper is a poem that takes, quite literally, a bird's-eye view.

The poet spies a jackdaw sitting on a weathervane on a church spire and imagines what the bird is looking down on – 'the bustle and the raree-show', the troubles that afflict humankind (the 'motley rout') but seem trivial and insignificant from the jackdaw's vantage point. Cowper ends by wishing he too could view the world from on high and envies the bird's freedom from earthly troubles and woes. This is a simple but elegant poem about reflecting on our priorities and understanding what really matters.

There is a bird who, by his coat,
And by the hoarseness of his note,
    Might be suppos'd a crow;
A great frequenter of the church,
Where, bishop-like, he finds a perch,
    And dormitory too.

Above the steeple shines a plate,
That turns and turns, to indicate
    From what point blows the weather.
Look up—your brains begin to swim,
'Tis in the clouds—that pleases him,
    He chooses it the rather.

Fond of the speculative height,
Thither he wings his airy flight,

    And thence securely sees
The bustle and the raree-show,
That occupy mankind below,
        Secure and at his ease.

You think, no doubt, he sits and muses
On future broken bones and bruises,
    If he should chance to fall.
No; not a single thought like that
Employs his philosophic pate,
    Or troubles it at all.

He sees, that this great roundabout—
The world, with all its motley rout,
    Church, army, physic, law,
Its customs, and its bus'nesses,
Is no concern at all of his,
      And says—what says he?—Caw.

Thrice happy bird! I too have seen
Much of the vanities of men;
    And, sick of having seen 'em,
Would cheerfully these limbs resign
For such a pair of wings as thine,
      And such a head between 'em.

CONDITION OR SITUATION:
The Horrors of War

PRESCRIPTION:
The Sleeper in the Valley (1870)
by Arthur Rimbaud

The horrors of war, or more pertinently trying to describe the horrors of war, has been the dark muse for many a poet, from Alfred, Lord Tennyson to Wilfred Owen. 'The Sleeper in the Valley' by Arthur Rimbaud is a deceptively peaceful poem that reveals the tragic reality of war through the image of a young soldier who appears to be sleeping in a lush, green valley. The poem begins with beautiful natural imagery, describing a sun-drenched hollow where wildflowers grow and a young man lies as if in peaceful slumber. However, this serene scene masks a darker truth, revealed only in the final line by 'two red holes' in his right side.

Rimbaud masterfully contrasts the beauty and indifference of nature with the brutality of war, emphasizing youth cut short by violence while also showing how nature continues its cycle regardless of human tragedy. The poem serves as a powerful anti-war statement, made more poignant by its subtle approach and dramatic revelation.

It's a green hollow where a river sings
Madly catching white tatters in the grass.
Where the sun on the proud mountain rings:
It's a little valley, foaming like light in a glass.

A conscript, open-mouthed, his bare head
And bare neck bathed in the cool blue cress,
Sleeps: stretched out, under the sky, on grass,
Pale where the light rains down on his green bed.

Feet in the yellow flags, he sleeps. Smiling
As a sick child might smile, he's dozing.
Nature, rock him warmly: he is cold.

The scents no longer make his nostrils twitch:
He sleeps in the sunlight, one hand on his chest,
Tranquil. In his right side, there are two red holes.

CONDITION OR SITUATION:
Questioning Faith

PRESCRIPTION:
On His Blindness (1673)
by John Milton

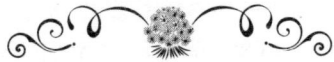

John Milton's 'On His Blindness' (also known as 'Sonnet 19' or 'When I Consider How My Light is Spent') grapples with the poet's anguish over losing his sight (Milton had been almost totally blind for a year when the poem was written) and its impact on his ability to serve God through his writing. The sonnet reveals Milton's initial despair and frustration at being unable to use his talent while living in darkness, fearing God's displeasure at his perceived inactivity.

The central tension lies between human ambition to serve, and divine expectations. Through a dialogue with Patience, Milton reaches a profound realization: God requires neither human labour nor gifts, but rather faith and acceptance.

The poem's transformative message concludes that serving God takes many forms, including patient endurance of suffering. The famous final line, 'They also serve who only stand and wait' offers consolation that passive acceptance and steadfast faith are equally valuable forms of divine service.

When I consider how my light is spent,
    Ere half my days, in this dark world and wide,
    And that one Talent which is death to hide
    Lodged with me useless, though my Soul more bent
To serve therewith my Maker, and present
    My true account, lest he returning chide;
    'Doth God exact day-labour, light denied?'
    I fondly ask. But patience, to prevent
That murmur, soon replies, 'God doth not need
    Either man's work or his own gifts; who best
    Bear his mild yoke, they serve him best. His state
Is Kingly. Thousands at his bidding speed
    And post o'er Land and Ocean without rest:
    They also serve who only stand and wait.'

CONDITION OR SITUATION:
Yearning for a Simple Life

PRESCRIPTION:
Ode on Solitude (c.1717)

by Alexander Pope

Ever found yourself yearning for 'the good life', free from the pressures and strife of modern living and social burdens?

Alexander Pope's serene poem, 'Ode on Solitude', celebrates the virtues of a simple, secluded life removed from society's ambitions and complications.

Written in his youth, the work envisions an ideal existence characterized by modest contentment, self-sufficiency and quiet contemplation. Pope portrays solitude not as isolation but as spiritual richness, where one lives on ancestral lands, enjoys honest labour, and maintains independence from worldly pursuits.

The poem elevates rural simplicity over urban complexity, suggesting that genuine happiness emerges from moderation rather than excess. Through measured quatrains, Pope creates a pastoral vision where health, study and inner peace flourish away from fame's corrupting influence.

His message affirms that true fulfilment comes from embracing life's essential pleasures – clean conscience, meaningful work and virtuous living – rather than chasing society's hollow rewards.

———————— ♦ ————————

Happy the man, whose wish and care
   A few paternal acres bound,
Content to breathe his native air,
         In his own ground.

Whose herds with milk, whose fields with bread,
   Whose flocks supply him with attire,
Whose trees in summer yield him shade,
         In winter fire.

Blest, who can unconcernedly find
                Hours, days, and years slide soft away,
In health of body, peace of mind,
            Quiet by day,

Sound sleep by night; study and ease,
   Together mixed; sweet recreation;
And innocence, which most does please,
               With meditation.

Thus let me live, unseen, unknown;
   Thus unlamented let me die;
Steal from the world, and not a stone
              Tell where I lie.

3

Remedies for the Mind

CONDITION OR SITUATION:
Feeling Gaslit by a Family Member

PRESCRIPTION:
We Remember Your Childhood Well (1990)
by Carol Ann Duffy

'We Remember Your Childhood Well' by Carol Ann Duffy is a disturbing poem that explores the theme of gaslighting and the denial of childhood trauma. The poem is written from the perspective of two parents responding to their grown child's memories of an unhappy childhood. Through a series of defensive denials, the parents attempt to rewrite and invalidate their child's traumatic memories.

The poem's key message is about how abusers often manipulate reality and deny their victims' experiences, creating a twisted version of events that serves their own narrative. The insistent tone of the parents reveals their attempt to maintain control through psychological manipulation. Duffy illustrates how memory and truth can be contested, particularly in family dynamics where power imbalances exist.

The title itself is ironic, as it becomes clear that the parents' version of remembering 'well' is actually a calculated erasure of the truth, highlighting the broader themes of power, abuse and the gaslighting of victims.

———————— ♦ ————————

Nobody hurt you. Nobody turned off the light and argued
with somebody else all night. The bad man on the moors
was only a movie you saw. Nobody locked the door.

Your questions were answered fully. No. That didn't occur.
You couldn't sing anyway, cared less. The moment's a blur, a Film Fun
laughing itself to death in the coal fire. Anyone's guess.

Nobody forced you. You wanted to go that day. Begged. You chose
the dress. Here are the pictures, look at you. Look at us all,
smiling and waving, younger. The whole thing is inside your head.

What you recall are impressions; we have the facts. We called the tune.
The secret police of your childhood were older and wiser than you, bigger
than you. Call back the sound of their voices. Boom. Boom. Boom.

Nobody sent you away. That was an extra holiday, with people
you seemed to like. They were firm, there was nothing to fear.
There was none but yourself to blame if it ended in tears.

What does it matter now? No, no, nobody left the skidmarks
   of sin
on your soul and laid you wide open for Hell. You were loved.
Always. We did what was best. We remember your childhood
   well.

CONDITION OR SITUATION:
Anger Management Issues

PRESCRIPTION:
A Poison Tree (1794)
by William Blake

'A Poison Tree' by William Blake conveys a powerful message about the dangers of suppressed anger and the destructive nature of hatred. The poem shows how anger, when expressed openly with a friend, dissolves naturally. However, when suppressed and nursed secretly (with an enemy), it grows into something toxic and deadly, symbolized by the poison apple in the poem.

Through simple but effective imagery of a tree growing from a seed of anger, Blake illustrates how negative emotions, when harboured and nurtured through deceit and false smiles, can lead to destructive outcomes.

The poem ends with the speaker's enemy lying dead beneath the tree, suggesting that unexpressed anger both destroys its target and also corrupts the person holding onto it. The central message warns against the dangers of repressing anger and the devastating consequences of allowing hatred to grow unchecked.

I was angry with my friend:
I told my wrath, my wrath did end.
I was angry with my foe:
I told it not, my wrath did grow.

And I watered it in fears
Night and morning with my tears,
And I sunned it with smiles
And with soft deceitful wiles.

And it grew both day and night,
Till it bore an apple bright,
And my foe beheld it shine,
And he knew that it was mine,—

And into my garden stole
When the night had veild the pole;
In the morning, glad, I see
My foe outstretched beneath the tree.

CONDITION OR SITUATION:
The Pain of Anticipation

PRESCRIPTION:
Hope (1846)
by Emily Brontë

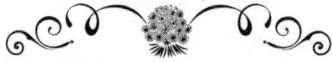

It is often said by people in the aftermath of a situation where the outcome has been a big disappointment that 'it is the hope that kills you' – a sentiment Emily Brontë would no doubt agree with. In Brontë's poem, Hope is personified as a 'timid friend' in the first stanza but as the poem progresses, she proves to be an unreliable and even heartless companion, 'cruel in her fear' and mocking the poet's sorrows and revelling in her disappointments.

Essentially, it's about the idea that having no hope can sometimes be less painful than having hope that is ultimately dashed. This is a common sentiment in situations where expectations are high, but so is the chance of failure, such as in sports competitions, relationships or personal goals.

Hope was but a timid friend;
    She sat without my grated den,
Watching how my fate would tend,
    Even as selfish-hearted men.

She was cruel in her fear;
   Through the bars one dreary day,
I looked out to see her there,
   And she turned her face away!

Like a false guard, false watch keeping,
   Still, in strife, she whispered peace;
She would sing while I was weeping;
   If I listened, she would cease.

False she was, and unrelenting;
   When my last joys strewed the ground,
Even Sorrow saw, repenting,
   Those sad relics scattered round;

Hope, whose whisper would have given
   Balm to all that frenzied pain,
Stretched her wings, and soared to heaven,
   Went, and ne'er returned again!

CONDITION OR SITUATION:
Building Resilience

PRESCRIPTION:
As I Grew Older (1926)
by Langston Hughes

'As I Grew Older' by Langston Hughes explores themes of racial oppression, perseverance and the struggle to maintain hope in the face of systemic barriers. The poem begins with the poet recalling a bright dream from their youth, symbolizing their early aspirations and ambitions. However, as time passes, a 'thick wall' rises between the poet and their dream, representing the racial discrimination and societal obstacles faced by African-Americans. The darkness of this wall threatens to overwhelm the poet's aspirations, yet the poem transitions into a message of determination and resistance.

Through the powerful imagery of breaking through the wall with their bare hands and reaching toward the light, Hughes conveys the necessity of fighting against oppression. The poem ultimately delivers a message about the resilience of the human spirit and the refusal to let racism and discrimination destroy dreams, even when those dreams become harder to reach.

It was a long time ago.
I have almost forgotten my dream.
But it was there then,
In front of me,
Bright like a sun,—
My dream.

And then the wall rose,
Rose slowly,
Slowly,
Between me and my dream.
Rose slowly, slowly,
Dimming,
Hiding,
The light of my dream.
Rose until it touched the sky,—
The wall.

Shadow.
I am black.

I lie down in the shadow.
No longer the light of my dream before me,
Above me.
Only the thick wall.
Only the shadow.

My hands!
My dark hands!
Break through the wall!

Find my dream!
Help me to shatter this darkness,
To smash this night,
To break this shadow
Into a thousand lights of sun,
Into a thousand whirling dreams
Of sun!

CONDITION OR SITUATION:

Contemplating the Inexorable Passing of Time and History

PRESCRIPTION:

Ozymandias (1818)

by Percy Bysshe Shelley

All things pass in time, and all great civilizations rise and fall. 'Ozymandias' explores themes of power, hubris and the inevitable decline of even the mightiest empires. Through the description of a broken statue in a desert, Shelley presents a profound meditation on the temporary nature of human power and achievement.

The poem centres on a fallen monument of an ancient king of Egypt, Ozymandias (an alternative name for Rameses

II), who proclaimed himself 'king of kings' and believed his works would endure forever. The irony lies in how his grand statue now lies shattered in the desert, destroyed by an earthquake with only 'two vast and trunkless legs of stone' and half of his face remaining. The surrounding barren and empty landscape emphasizes how time and nature have completely erased his once-great empire.

Shelley's poignant central message is that all human power, pride and achievements are ultimately fleeting. No matter how mighty or important we consider ourselves, time will eventually erase all traces of our existence. The poem serves as a warning against arrogance and as a reminder of mortality, suggesting that nature and time are the only true eternal powers.

I met a traveller from an antique land
Who said: 'Two vast and trunkless legs of stone
Stand in the desert ... Near them, on the sand,
Half sunk, a shattered visage lies, whose frown,
And wrinkled lip, and sneer of cold command,
Tell that its sculptor well those passions read
Which yet survive, stamped on these lifeless things,
The hand that mocked them, and the heart that fed:
And on the pedestal these words appear:
"My name is Ozymandias, king of kings:
Look on my works, ye Mighty, and despair!"
Nothing beside remains. Round the decay
Of that colossal wreck, boundless and bare
The lone and level sands stretch far away.'

CONDITION OR SITUATION:
Feeling Lost for Words

PRESCRIPTION:
Cascando (1936)

by Samuel Beckett

Sometimes it's hard to find the right words to express what is raging in our hearts and minds; the limitations of language become an oppressive burden. Beckett's haunting poem 'Cascando' explores the tension between language and authentic expression, portraying a speaker caught in the cycle of articulating love while doubting words' ability to convey genuine emotion. The title itself – suggesting a falling – mirrors the poem's structure as it tumbles toward silence.

Throughout 'Cascando', Beckett juxtaposes the compulsion to speak against the recognition of language's ultimate inadequacy, creating a meditation on how words simultaneously reveal and obscure truth. The recurring phrases and fragmented structure reflect the speaker's struggle to find meaning in repetition and pattern, even as these patterns break down. At its core, the poem examines the paradoxical human need to express the inexpressible, suggesting that in the gaps between words – in what remains unsaid – more profound truths might reside.

1

why not merely the despaired of
occasion of
wordshed
is it not better abort than be barren

the hours after you are gone are so leaden
they will always start dragging too soon
the grapples clawing blindly the bed of want
bringing up the bones the old loves
sockets filled once with eyes like yours
all always is it better too soon than never
the black want splashing their faces
saying again nine days never floated the loved
nor nine months
nor nine lives

2

saying again
if you do not teach me I shall not learn
saying again there is a last
even of last times
last times of begging
last times of loving
of knowing not knowing pretending
a last even of last times of saying
if you do not love me I shall not be loved
if I do not love you I shall not love

the churn of stale words in the heart again
love love love thud of the old plunger
pestling the unalterable
whey of words
terrified again
of not loving
of loving and not you
of being loved and not by you
of knowing not knowing pretending
pretending
I and all the others that will love you
if they love you

3
unless they love you

CONDITION OR SITUATION:
Understanding Life's Dualities

PRESCRIPTION:
Stonepicker (2001)

by Frieda Hughes

Artist and writer Frieda Hughes is familiar with emotional fortitude in the face of adversity, having lost both her mother – the poet Sylvia Plath – and later her brother in tragic circumstances.

In 'Stonepicker', she examines the themes of endurance and survival. Picking stones, a relentless task, acts as a metaphor for dealing with emotional burdens. The toil does not leave her unscathed, however, and she is 'scooped out and bow-like'. But, as she works through the task, she becomes stronger. The stones are both heavy weights and weapons of survival, showing that hardship can become strength and resilience.

She is scooped out and bow-like,
As if her string
Has been drawn tight.

But really, she is
Plucking stones from the dirt
For her shoulder-bag.

It is her dead albatross,
Her cross, her choice,
In it lie her weapons.

Each granite sphere
Or sea-worn flint
Has weight against your sin,

You cannot win.
She calls you close,
But not to let you in, only

For a better aim.

CONDITION OR SITUATION:
Coping with Disappointment

PRESCRIPTION:
A Dream Lies Dead (1928)

by Dorothy Parker

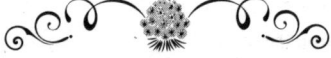

Dorothy Parker's 'A Dream Lies Dead' explores themes of lost hope, disillusionment and emotional detachment through the metaphor of a dead dream. The poem portrays the speaker's surprisingly calm acceptance of shattered aspirations, creating a striking contrast between the gravity of loss and the speaker's almost indifferent response. Is this emotional numbness, or perhaps a defensive mechanism against pain?

The irony lies in how the speaker refuses to perform traditional rituals of grief, choosing instead to leave the dream where it fell. This seemingly cold response masks deeper emotions and hints at past hurts that have taught the speaker to protect themselves from emotional investment.

The overall message reflects Parker's cynicism: sometimes the death of hopes or dreams is met not with dramatic sorrow but with quiet resignation, highlighting how people adapt to disappointment through emotional distance.

A dream lies dead here. May you softly go
Before this place, and turn away your eyes,
Nor seek to know the look of that which dies
Importuning Life for life. Walk not in woe,
But, for a little, let your step be slow.
And, of your mercy, be not sweetly wise
With words of hope and Spring and tenderer skies.
A dream lies dead; and this all mourners know:

Whenever one drifted petal leaves the tree —
Though white of bloom as it had been before
And proudly waitful of fecundity —
One little loveliness can be no more;
And so must Beauty bow her imperfect head
Because a dream has joined the wistful dead!

CONDITION OR SITUATION:
Peaceful Retrospection

PRESCRIPTION:
I Sit Beside the Fire and Think (1954)
by J. R. R. Tolkien

This contemplative poem explores themes of memory, aging and the passage of time. Tolkien creates a reflective atmosphere as the speaker sits by the fireplace, musing on past adventures. The poem weaves together thoughts of both grand experiences (mountains, kingdoms) and simple pleasures (spring, autumn leaves), suggesting that all memories hold significance. The recurring imagery of seasons and natural elements emphasizes life's cyclical nature and the inevitable flow of time. There's a gentle melancholy in the speaker's reflection, yet also a sense of contentment and acceptance.

Tolkien suggests that as we age, our memories become precious treasures that we can revisit in quiet moments, and that there's beauty in this contemplative stage of life. The overall tone is one of peaceful retrospection rather than regret or sadness.

I sit beside the fire and think of all that I have seen,
of meadow-flowers and butterflies in summers that have been;

Of yellow leaves and gossamer in autumns that there were,
with morning mist and silver sun and wind upon my hair.
I sit beside the fire and think of how the world will be
when winter comes without a spring that I shall ever see.

For still there are so many things that I have never seen:
in every wood in every spring there is a different green.
I sit beside the fire and think of people long ago,
and people who will see a world that I shall never know.
But all the while I sit and think of times there were before,
I listen for returning feet and voices at the door.

CONDITION OR SITUATION:
Understanding Depressive Illness

PRESCRIPTION:
A Life (c.1965)

by Sylvia Plath

A deeply distressing poem, 'A Life' explores the profound isolation and detachment that can accompany existence, especially under the weight of depression. The poem presents life as an exhibit behind glass, in a painting or trapped inside a bauble – strange, fragile and ultimately unreachable –

emphasizing a sense of alienation from both the self and the world.

Through vivid metaphors, Plath communicates how depression renders ordinary experiences and emotions distant and artificial. The recurring motifs of stillness, artifice and suffocating routine serve to underscore the numbing effect of mental illness, illustrating how depression transforms life into a spectacle observed rather than lived.

Essentially, the poem reflects on the painful invisibility and voicelessness that those suffering from depression often endure, suggesting a desperate longing for genuine connection and vitality in the face of overwhelming emptiness. Plath's work powerfully conveys the inner reality of depression as silent, isolating and deeply misunderstood. 'A Life' is thought to be a reflection on the time Plath spent in hospital recuperating after a failed suicide attempt in 1953.

Touch it: it won't shrink like an eyeball,
This egg-shaped bailiwick, clear as a tear.
Here's yesterday, last year—
Palm-spear and lily distinct as flora in the vast
Windless threadwork of a tapestry.

Flick the glass with your fingernail:
It will ping like a Chinese chime in the slightest air stir
Though nobody in there looks up or bothers to answer.
The inhabitants are light as cork,
Every one of them permanently busy.

At their feet, the sea waves bow in single file.
Never trespassing in bad temper:
Stalling in midair,
Short-reined, pawing like paradeground horses.
Overhead, the clouds sit tasseled and fancy

As Victorian cushions. This family
Of valentine faces might please a collector:
They ring true, like good china.

Elsewhere the landscape is more frank.
The light falls without letup, blindingly.

A woman is dragging her shadow in a circle
About a bald hospital saucer.
It resembles the moon, or a sheet of blank paper
And appears to have suffered a sort of private blitzkrieg.
She lives quietly

With no attachments, like a foetus in a bottle,
The obsolete house, the sea, flattened to a picture
She has one too many dimensions to enter.
Grief and anger, exorcised,
Leave her alone now.

The future is a grey seagull
Tattling in its cat-voice of departure.
Age and terror, like nurses, attend her,
And a drowned man, complaining of the great cold,
Crawls up out of the sea.

CONDITION OR SITUATION:
Overcome by Lustful Desires

PRESCRIPTION:
Down, Wanton, Down! (1933)
by Robert Graves

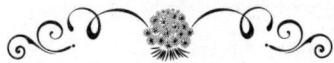

'Down, Wanton, Down!' by Robert Graves is a stern self-address that explores the conflict between sexual desire and rational control. The poem presents an internal dialogue where the speaker attempts to subdue and reason with their own lustful impulses. Through personification of desire as a 'wanton' that needs taming, Graves examines the age-old struggle between physical passion and intellectual restraint.

The poem suggests that unchecked sexual desire can lead to destruction and foolishness, while also acknowledging its powerful and persistent nature. Using almost songlike language and tone, the speaker argues that human dignity and reason should triumph over base instincts. The work reflects broader themes about the relationship between mind and body, self-control, and the potential consequences of giving in to physical temptation. Ultimately, the poem serves as a cautionary reminder about maintaining control over one's baser instincts.

Down, wanton, down! Have you no shame
That at the whisper of Love's name,
Or Beauty's, presto! up you raise
Your angry head and stand at gaze?

Poor Bombard-captain, sworn to reach
The ravelin and effect a breach –
Indifferent what you storm or why,
So be that in the breach you die!

Love may be blind, but Love at least
Knows what is man and what mere beast;
Or Beauty wayward, but requires
More delicacy from her squires.

Tell me, my witless, whose one boast
Could be your staunchness at the post,
When were you made a man of parts
To think fine and profess the arts?

Will many-gifted Beauty come
Bowing to your bald rule of thumb,
Or Love swear loyalty to your crown?
Be gone, have done! Down, wanton, down!

CONDITION OR SITUATION:
Writer's Block

PRESCRIPTION:
February (1912)
by Boris Pasternak

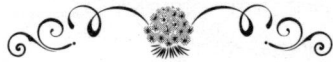

All writers suffer from writer's block from time to time and yearn for a spark of inspiration. 'February' by Boris Pasternak explores the profound connection between creative expression, natural cycles and emotional turmoil. The poem portrays spring not as a time of renewal and joy, but as a dark, overwhelming force that demands the poet's full emotional attention.

Pasternak suggests that true artistic experience requires the poet to abandon the act of writing to fully immerse themself in raw feeling and natural phenomena. The poem emphasizes how nature's awakening can mirror and trigger deep personal emotions, making the act of writing seem inadequate or artificial in comparison.

Through vivid imagery of almost apocalyptic intensity, the poem argues that some experiences are too powerful to be captured by pen and paper, and must instead be lived and felt completely. The message ultimately celebrates the primacy of direct emotional experience over artistic documentation, while acknowledging the powerful impact of seasonal change on human consciousness.

Black spring! Pick up your pen, and weeping,
Of February, in sobs and ink,
Write poems, while the slush in thunder
Is burning in the black of spring.

Through clanking wheels, through church bells ringing
A hired cab will take you where
The town has ended, where the showers
Are louder still than ink and tears.

Where rooks, like charred pears, from the branches
In thousands break away, and sweep
Into the melting snow, instilling
Dry sadness into eyes that weep.

Beneath—the earth is black in puddles,
The wind with croaking screeches throbs,
And—the more randomly, the surer
Poems are forming out of sobs.

CONDITION OR SITUATION:
Saying What You Should Have Said at the Time

PRESCRIPTION:
Lasagne (2013)
by Brendan Cleary

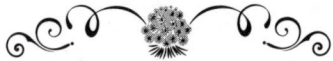

We all know that awkward feeling of biting our tongue when someone has gone to the trouble of cooking us a meal and we have not enjoyed it.

This situation is magnified in relationships, especially ones that may contain a fair amount of emotional insecurity or volatility. Of course, in the aftermath of a relationship, when all second bets, not to mention the gloves, are resolutely off, some home truths can be aired – a situation poignantly observed by Northern Irish poet Brendan Cleary in his simple if slightly melancholy poem 'Lasagne', which firmly puts the record straight even as the last line betrays a stilted sadness.

There's something
I've wanted to tell you,
even when we were together,
but I thought it better
I kept it to myself.
Yes, my love,

it's regarding your Lasagne,
it was always too dry
but I didn't want to tell you
or mention it at the time.
Thought I'd put you in the picture
now that you've gone
& are cooking Lasagne
without much liquid
for somebody else.

CONDITION OR SITUATION:
Experiencing Déjà Vu

PRESCRIPTION:
Sudden Light (1881)

by Dante Gabriel Rossetti

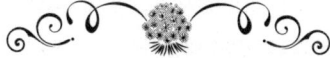

Ever have the feeling you have been somewhere before, in body or in mind? 'Sudden Light' by Dante Gabriel Rossetti explores themes of reincarnation, eternal love and spiritual déjà vu. The poem captures a moment of transcendent recognition where the poet experiences a profound sense of having lived this exact moment before. Through lyrical imagery and gentle repetition, Rossetti suggests that love transcends single lifetimes, recurring across multiple existences. The poet creates an atmosphere of mystical familiarity, where present experiences echo with past lives and future possibilities.

The poem's central focus is on the eternal nature of true love and its ability to bridge different times and incarnations. By describing familiar sensations – the scent of grass, the tilt of a head – the poem suggests that deep connections between souls persist through time. The message ultimately affirms the immortality of love and the interconnectedness of past and present experiences, offering comfort in the idea that genuine love is never truly lost.

I have been here before,
But when or how I cannot tell:
I know the grass beyond the door,
The sweet keen smell,
The sighing sound, the lights around the shore.

You have been mine before,
How long ago I may not know:
But just when at that swallow's soar
Your neck turned so,
Some veil did fall – I knew it all of yore.

Has this been thus before?
And shall not thus time's eddying flight
Still with our lives our love restore
In death's despite,
And day and night yield one delight once more?

CONDITION OR SITUATION:
Being Hard on Yourself

PRESCRIPTION:
Things (1979)
by Fleur Adcock

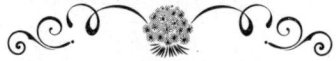

Fleur Adcock is known for her conversational yet insightful poetry. She writes with an observational style that is clear and straightforward. In her poem 'Things', she addresses the subject of the insomniac's anxiety and, indeed, many will recognize the familiar rhythm of whirling thoughts – the trivial and the meaningful together, chewed over endlessly by a vulnerable and overtired brain. It is comforting at the end of the poem when 'All the worse things come stalking in and stand icily about the bed' – by drawing attention to these 'worse things', to the universal worries, Adcock renders them harmless, leaving the reader relieved and ready to sleep. Perhaps one for the bedside table.

There are worse things than having behaved foolishly in public.
There are worse things than these miniature betrayals,
committed or endured or suspected; there are worse things
than not being able to sleep for thinking about them.
It is 5 a.m. All the worse things come stalking in
and stand icily about the bed looking worse and worse
   and worse.

CONDITION OR SITUATION:
How to Preserve Memories

PRESCRIPTION:
The Treasure (c.1915)
by Rupert Brooke

Ah, the follies of youth and those rose-tinted spectacles we often slip on to view our memories. 'The Treasure' by Rupert Brooke contemplates the enduring beauty and value of youthful dreams and memories.

The poem celebrates the inner riches carried by individuals – moments of joy, hope and youthful wonder – that remain untouched by time or external hardships. For Brooke these treasured experiences are a source of comfort and inspiration, even in times of suffering or uncertainty. He emphasizes the contrast between the fleeting nature of life and the more enduring essence of such memories, implying that true wealth is not found in material possessions but in the cherished moments that make life meaningful.

When colour goes home into the eyes,
And lights that shine are shut again
With dancing girls and sweet birds' cries
Behind the gateways of the brain;
And that no-place which gave them birth, shall close

The rainbow and the rose:
Still may Time hold some golden space
Where I'll unpack that scented store
Of song and flower and sky and face,
And count, and touch, and turn them o'er,
Musing upon them; as a mother, who
Has watched her children all the rich day through
Sits, quiet-handed, in the fading light,
When children sleep, ere night.

CONDITION OR SITUATION:
Understanding a Strong Work Ethic

PRESCRIPTION:
Work (1850)
by Elizabeth Barrett Browning

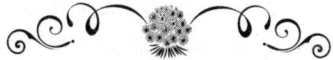

If you have ever been in a situation where you felt that life is all work and no play, spare a thought for Elizabeth Barrett Browning's view of the sanctity of labour. Her poem, 'Work', written in characteristic sonnet form, explores the dignity, purpose and moral value found in honest toil.

The poem reflects on how meaningful work connects individuals to both the divine and the broader human community, suggesting that labour is a form of worship and contribution to society. Browning emphasizes that work, whether humble or grand, possesses inherent worth when performed with sincerity and dedication.

She challenges the notion that only celebrated achievements matter, highlighting instead the spiritual fulfilment and character growth that result from persistent effort.

What are we set on earth for? Say, to toil;
Nor seek to leave thy tending of the vines
For all the heat o' the day, till it declines,
And Death's mild curfew shall from work assoil.
God did anoint thee with his odorous oil,
To wrestle, not to reign; and He assigns
All thy tears over, like pure crystallines,
For younger fellow-workers of the soil
To wear for amulets. So others shall
Take patience, labour, to their heart and hand
From thy hand and thy heart and thy brave cheer,
And God's grace fructify through thee to
The least flower with a brimming cup may stand,
And share its dew-drop with another near.

CONDITION OR SITUATION:
Fragile Relationships

PRESCRIPTION:
Keeping Orchids (2007)
by Jackie Kay

Jackie Kay, a former Scots Makar (Scottish Poet Laureate), draws upon her own personal experience of the complex nature of family and identity to shape her writing, giving it a distinctive honesty and emotional depth.

In this poem, Kay, who was adopted as a child, reflects on the first time she met her birth mother. The orchids – a gift from her mother – are symbolic of the emotions stirred up by this encounter. As the flowers fade, so does her hope for connection with her mother, leaving behind a lingering sense of disappointment and fragmented memories of an awkward meeting.

The poem examines complex mother-daughter relationships and the struggle to understand each other. It explores the challenges of intergenerational relationships, encouraging us to appreciate their complexity and the difficulties of keeping connections across different ages and versions of ourselves.

The orchids my mother gave me when we first met
are still alive, twelve days later. Although

some of the buds remain closed as secrets.
Twice since I carried them back, like a baby in a shawl,

from her train station to mine, then home. Twice
since then the whole glass carafe has crashed

falling over, unprovoked, soaking my chest of drawers.
All the broken waters. I have rearranged

the upset orchids with troubled hands. Even after
that the closed ones did not open out. The skin

shut like an eye in the dark; the closed lid.
Twelve days later, my mother's hands are all I have.

Her voice is fading fast. Even her voice rushes
through a tunnel the other way from home.

I close my eyes and try to remember exactly:
a paisley pattern scarf, a brooch, a navy coat.

A digital watch her daughter was wearing when she died.
Now they hang their heads,

and suddenly grow old – the proof of meeting. Still,
her hands, awkward and hard to hold

fold and unfold a green carrier bag as she tells
the story of her life. Compressed. Airtight.

A sad square, then a crumpled shape. A bag of tricks.
Her secret life – a hidden album, a box of love letters.

A door opens and closes. Time is outside waiting.
I catch the draught in my winter room.

Airlocks keep the cold air out.
Boiling water makes flowers live longer. So does

cutting the stems with a sharp knife.

CONDITION OR SITUATION:
Inspiration Interrupted

PRESCRIPTION:
Kubla Khan (1816)

by Samuel Taylor Coleridge

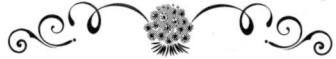

Literary legend has it that Coleridge started composing 'Kubla Khan' while in the midst of a laudanum-inspired dream when he was rudely interrupted by 'a person on business from Porlock', who detained him for some time. The opium vision faded, leaving the poem unfinished.

The poem presents the mystical palace of Xanadu set within a rich, almost supernatural landscape, blending beauty with a sense of threat and mystery. Coleridge delves into the power of artistic vision and the complex process of creativity, suggesting that the imagination can conjure worlds as vivid and profound as reality itself, yet these visions remain fragile and elusive.

The dreamlike atmosphere emphasizes the tension between order and chaos, as well as the longing for transcendence through art. Ultimately, the poem's message lies in its celebration of creative inspiration and its acknowledgement of the transient, sometimes unattainable, nature of our most powerful imaginings. Through this, Coleridge highlights both the potential and limits of human creativity. I believe it can be summed up by one single word in the first stanza: 'measureless' – now that, ladies and gentlemen, is what poetry is all about.

Or, a Vision in a Dream. A Fragment.
In Xanadu did Kubla Khan
A stately pleasure dome decree:
Where Alph, the sacred river, ran
Through caverns measureless to man
    Down to a sunless sea.
So twice five miles of fertile ground
With walls and towers were girdled round:
And there were gardens bright with sinuous rills,
Where blossomed many an incense-bearing tree;
And here were forests ancient as the hills,
Enfolding sunny spots of greenery.

But oh! that deep romantic chasm which slanted
Down the green hill athwart a cedarn cover!
A savage place! as holy and enchanted
As e'er beneath a waning moon was haunted
By woman wailing for her demon lover!
And from this chasm, with ceaseless turmoil seething,
As if this earth in fast thick pants were breathing,
A mighty fountain momently was forced:
Amid whose swift half-intermitted burst
Huge fragments vaulted like rebounding hail,
Or chaffy grain beneath the thresher's flail:
And 'mid these dancing rocks at once and ever
It flung up momently the sacred river.
Five miles meandering with a mazy motion
Through wood and dale the sacred river ran,
Then reached the caverns measureless to man,
And sank in tumult to a lifeless ocean:
And 'mid this tumult Kubla heard from far
Ancestral voices prophesying war!

   The shadow of the dome of pleasure
    Floated midway on the waves;
   Where was heard the mingled measure
    From the fountain and the caves.
It was a miracle of rare device,
A sunny pleasure dome with caves of ice!

   A damsel with a dulcimer
   In a vision once I saw:
   It was an Abyssinian maid
   And on her dulcimer she played,

    Singing of Mount Abora.
    Could I revive within me
    Her symphony and song,
    To such a deep delight 'twould win me,
That with music loud and long,
I would build that dome in air,
That sunny dome! those caves of ice!
And all who heard should see them there,
And all should cry, Beware! Beware!
His flashing eyes, his floating hair!
Weave a circle round him thrice,
And close your eyes with holy dread,
For he on honey-dew hath fed,
And drunk the milk of Paradise.

CONDITION OR SITUATION:
In Need of a Change of Perspective

PRESCRIPTION:
Thirteen Ways of Looking at a Blackbird (1917)

by Wallace Stevens

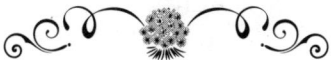

Sometimes all that is needed is a change of perspective. 'Thirteen Ways of Looking at a Blackbird' by Wallace Stevens is a modernist masterpiece that explores multiple perspectives of reality through thirteen distinct stanzas, each presenting a different way of observing and understanding a blackbird. He challenges traditional modes of perception by demonstrating how this single subject can be viewed and interpreted in various ways.

Stevens uses the blackbird as a metaphor to explore larger philosophical questions about consciousness, reality and the relationship between the observer and the observed. Through stark imagery and precise language, the poem suggests that truth is not singular but multifaceted, and our understanding of reality depends on our perspective and context.

Stevens argues that meaning and reality are fluid, subjective experiences, and true understanding comes from acknowledging multiple viewpoints rather than seeking a single, definitive interpretation. The poem celebrates the complexity of perception and the richness of multiple perspectives.

I
Among twenty snowy mountains,
The only moving thing
Was the eye of the black bird.

II
I was of three minds,
Like a tree
In which there are three blackbirds.

III
The blackbird whirled in the autumn winds.
It was a small part of the pantomime.

IV
A man and a woman
Are one.
A man and a woman and a blackbird
Are one.

V
I do not know which to prefer,
The beauty of inflections
Or the beauty of innuendoes,
The blackbird whistling
Or just after.

VI

Icicles filled the long window
With barbaric glass.
The shadow of the blackbird
Crossed it, to and fro.
The mood
Traced in the shadow
An indecipherable cause.

VII

O thin men of Haddam,
Why do you imagine golden birds?
Do you not see how the blackbird
Walks around the feet
Of the women about you?

VIII

I know noble accents
And lucid, inescapable rhythms;
But I know, too,
That the blackbird is involved
In what I know.

IX

When the blackbird flew out of sight,
It marked the edge
Of one of many circles.

X

At the sight of blackbirds

Flying in a green light,
Even the bawds of euphony
Would cry out sharply.

XI
He rode over Connecticut
In a glass coach.
Once, a fear pierced him,
In that he mistook
The shadow of his equipage
For blackbirds.

XII
The river is moving.
The blackbird must be flying.

XIII
It was evening all afternoon.
It was snowing
And it was going to snow.
The blackbird sat
In the cedar-limbs.

4

Remedies for the Self and Others

CONDITION OR SITUATION:
In Need of Solidarity

PRESCRIPTION:
No Man Is an Island (1624)
by John Donne

'No Man Is an Island' by John Donne emphasizes the interconnectedness of all humanity and the profound impact each person's life and death has on others. He wrote the poem in the early seventeenth century, at a time of frequent epidemics when disease and death were an unwelcome if accepted part of everyday life. Through this piece, the common feelings of anxiety and dread are turned into a more comforting shared human experience.

The poem argues against the notion of complete self-sufficiency, asserting that humans are not isolated entities but rather pieces of a larger whole, figuratively described as parts of a continent. Donne uses powerful metaphors comparing humanity to a landmass where each person's death diminishes the whole, just as Europe would be lessened by the loss of a piece of land.

The tolling of the funeral bell serves as a reminder that everyone's death affects the entire community, leading to the famous conclusion: 'And therefore never send to know for whom the bell tolls; It tolls for thee.'

The poem's central message is that human beings are inherently social creatures who depend on and affect one another, making compassion and social responsibility essential aspects of life.

No man is an island,
Entire of itself;
Every man is a piece of the continent,
A part of the main.

If a clod be washed away by the sea,
Europe is the less,
As well as if a promontory were:
As well as if a manor of thy friend's
Or of thine own were.

Any man's death diminishes me,
Because I am involved in mankind.
And therefore never send to know
   for whom the bell tolls;
It tolls for thee.

CONDITION OR SITUATION:
Inspiring Hope for a Better World

PRESCRIPTION:
Where the Mind Is Without Fear (1910)
by Rabindranath Tagore

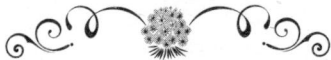

'Where the Mind is Without Fear' by Rabindranath Tagore presents a powerful vision of freedom and national awakening, written during India's struggle for independence in the first half of the twentieth century. Sadly, Tagore himself did not live to experience the end of British rule as he died in 1941, a full six years before India's dream of independence became reality.

The poem envisions an ideal world where people can live with dignity, knowledge and truth, free from the constraints of colonialism and social barriers.

Tagore emphasizes the importance of reason over superstition, unity over division and the pursuit of perfection through tireless effort. He dreams of a world where knowledge flows freely, where narrow domestic walls of prejudice and discrimination don't divide people, and where words of truth spring from the depths of the heart.

The poem is a prayer for awakening into a world of freedom – not just political, but intellectual and spiritual liberation.

Through these aspirations, Tagore communicates the universal desire for human dignity and the need to break free from mental and social chains that restrict human potential.

———————————— ♦ ————————————

Where the mind is without fear and the head is held high;
   Where knowledge is free;
   Where the world has not been broken up into fragments by narrow domestic walls;
   Where words come out from the depth of truth;
   Where tireless striving stretches its arms towards perfection;
   Where the clear stream of reason has not lost its way into the dreary desert sand of dead habit;
   Where the mind is led forward by thee into ever-widening thought and action
   Into that heaven of freedom, my Father, let my country awake.

CONDITION OR SITUATION:
The Difference Between Inner Feelings and Outward Appearances

PRESCRIPTION:
Not Waving but Drowning (1957)
by Stevie Smith

'Not Waving but Drowning' is the title poem of the 1957 poetry collection by British poet Florence Margaret Smith, perhaps better known by her nickname, Stevie Smith. This, her most famous and distinctive poem, is a haunting and powerful piece that explores themes of isolation, miscommunication and the disconnect between public perception and private suffering. The poem centres on a man who has died by drowning after his distress signals were mistaken for friendly waves by onlookers.

Smith uses this tragic misunderstanding to illustrate how people often overlook others' emotional pain, mistaking distress for well-being. The phrase 'I was much too far out all my life' suggests a long-term struggle with isolation that others failed to notice.

The message emphasizes how people can be suffering deeply while appearing fine to others, highlighting society's inability or unwillingness to recognize genuine distress. The poem serves as a commentary on human communication and connection, suggesting that we often miss the true meaning behind others' actions and gestures, sometimes with the most devastating consequences.

Nobody heard him, the dead man,
But still he lay moaning:
I was much further out than you thought
And not waving but drowning.

Poor chap, he always loved larking
And now he's dead
It must have been too cold for him
   his heart gave way,
They said.

Oh, no no no, it was too cold always
(Still the dead one lay moaning)
I was much too far out all my life
And not waving but drowning.

CONDITION OR SITUATION:
The Process of Aging

PRESCRIPTION:
Growing Old (1867)
by Matthew Arnold

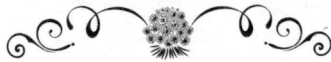

Matthew Arnold's 'Growing Old' presents a stark and unsentimental view of aging, stripping away romantic notions about the twilight years of life. The poem explores the harsh realities of physical and mental decline, describing aging not as a gentle transition but as a process of loss and diminishment.

Arnold emphasizes how aging brings the fading of passion, strength and beauty, along with the erosion of life's pleasures and possibilities. The poem challenges conventional comforting narratives about wisdom and serenity in old age, instead portraying it as a time of increasing isolation and limitation.

With direct and sometimes brutal honesty, Arnold suggests that growing old is primarily about what we lose rather than what we gain, and that aging is an inevitable process of deterioration that must be faced with clear-eyed realism rather than comfortable illusions about golden years or accumulated wisdom.

What is it to grow old?
Is it to lose the glory of the form,
The lustre of the eye?
Is it for beauty to forego her wreath?
Yes, but not for this alone.

Is it to feel our strength,
Not our bloom only, but our strength, decay?
Is it to feel each limb
Grow stiffer, every function less exact,
Each nerve more weakly strung?

Yes, this, and more! but not,
Ah, 'tis not what in youth we dreamed 'twould be!
'Tis not to have our life
Mellowed and softened as with sunset glow,
A golden day's decline!

'Tis not to see the world
As from a height, with rapt prophetic eyes,
And heart profoundly stirred;
And weep, and feel the fullness of the past,
The years that are no more!

It is to spend long days
And not once feel that we were ever young.
It is to add, immured
In the hot prison of the present, month
To month with weary pain.

It is to suffer this,
And feel but half, and feebly, what we feel:
Deep in our hidden heart
Festers the dull remembrance of a change,
But no emotion – none.

It is last stage of all,
When we are frozen up within, and quite
The phantom of ourselves,
To hear the world applaud the hollow ghost
Which blamed the living man.

CONDITION OR SITUATION:
Childhood Innocence

PRESCRIPTION:
I Was a Child in the World of the Powerful (c.1931)
by Osip Mandelstam

Adult life can be harsh, and it certainly was for Russian poet Osip Mandelstam, caught up in the chaos of the Russian Revolution and later persecuted under the Great Purges of the Stalin's Soviet regime. In his poem 'I Was a Child in the World of the Powerful', Mandelstam finds himself lost in a space between the bourgeoisie, which he neither understood nor embraced as a child, and the more sinister, powerful influences of post-revolutionary Russia.

The reference to Nereids, mythical sea nymphs of classical Greek mythology, suggests the sanctuary he sought in the innocence of his childhood imagination.

———————— ◆ ————————

I was a child in the world of the powerful.
I was frightened of oysters and looked at guardsmen
    distrustfully.
I am not bound to it by even the tiniest fragment of my soul
no matter how much I once tormented myself to be part
    of it.

I did not pose under the Egyptian portico of the bank,
self-importantly in a fur hat,
and the gypsy girl never ever danced for me, to the crackle
of 100 rouble notes beside the lemon yellow Neva.

I took so much embarrassment, stress and grief
from the tender Europeanised beauties of my past,
and sensing future executions I escaped from the roar of
    revolution
to the Nereids by the Black Sea.

So why does this city have the right
to dominate my thoughts and feelings to this day?

Fires and frost have made it even more brazen,
arrogant, cursed, empty and youthful.

Is it because I once saw a children's picture
of Lady Godiva with her red mane of hair?
I still whisper to myself again and again:
'Farewell Lady Godiva, Godiva, it's all over ... '

CONDITION OR SITUATION:
Balancing Duty and Desire

PRESCRIPTION:
The Conflict (c.1786)

by Friedrich Schiller

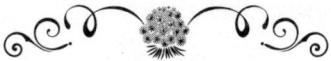

'The Conflict' by Friedrich Schiller explores the eternal struggle between duty and desire, focusing on the internal battle between moral obligations and personal passions. The poem delves into the challenging choices individuals face when their hearts' desires conflict with their moral responsibilities.

Schiller portrays this struggle through powerful imagery of internal warfare, depicting how humans are torn between their sensual nature and ethical principles. The poem suggests that this conflict is not merely personal but universal to the human condition, representing the ongoing tension between what we want and what we ought to do.

The poet's message emphasizes that true nobility lies not in the complete victory of duty over desire, but in the continuous effort to maintain balance between these opposing forces. Through this exploration, Schiller suggests that human dignity and growth come from acknowledging and managing this eternal conflict rather than attempting to eliminate it entirely.

No! I this conflict longer will not wage,
The conflict duty claims the giant task;
Thy spells, O virtue, never can assuage
The heart's wild fire this offering do not ask

True, I have sworn a solemn vow have sworn,
That I myself will curb the self within;
Yet take thy wreath, no more it shall be worn
Take back thy wreath, and leave me free to sin.

Rent be the contract I with thee once made;
She loves me, loves me forfeit be the crown!
Blessed he who, lulled in rapture's dreamy shade,
Glides, as I glide, the deep fall gladly down.

She sees the worm that my youth's bloom decays,
She sees my spring-time wasted as it flees;
And, marvelling at the rigor that gainsays
The heart's sweet impulse, my reward decrees.

Distrust this angel purity, fair soul!
It is to guilt thy pity armeth me;
Could being lavish its unmeasured whole,
It ne'er could give a gift to rival thee!

Thee the dear guilt I ever seek to shun,
O tyranny of fate, O wild desires!
My virtue's only crown can but be won
In that last breath when virtue's self expires!

CONDITION OR SITUATION:
The Pain of Parenthood

PRESCRIPTION:
Walking Away (1962)

by Cecil Day-Lewis

In 'Walking Away', Cecil Day-Lewis presents a poignant reflection on parenthood and the bittersweet experience of watching a child grow toward independence. The poem describes a specific memory of the poet watching his son walk away after a school football match, using this moment as a metaphor for the gradual process of letting go.

Through delicate and emotive language, Day-Lewis explores

the universal parental experience of witnessing their child's journey toward autonomy. The poet captures the mixture of pride and pain that accompanies this natural progression, describing it as both 'selfless' and 'self-hurting'. His imagery of the son's figure 'growing smaller' powerfully symbolizes the increasing distance between parent and child.

The poem's central message emphasizes that true parental love involves the courage to allow children their freedom, even when it causes personal anguish. Day-Lewis suggests that this separation is both necessary and natural, representing a fundamental truth about love and parenthood.

It is eighteen years ago, almost to the day –
A sunny day with leaves just turning,
The touch-lines new-ruled – since I watched you play
Your first game of football, then, like a satellite
Wrenched from its orbit, go drifting away
Behind a scatter of boys. I can see
You walking away from me towards the school
With the pathos of a half-fledged thing set free
Into a wilderness, the gait of one
Who finds no path where the path should be.
That hesitant figure, eddying away
Like a winged seed loosened from its parent stem,
Has something I never quite grasp to convey
About nature's give-and-take – the small, the scorching
Ordeals which fire one's irresolute clay.
I have had worse partings, but none that so
Gnaws at my mind still. Perhaps it is roughly

Saying what God alone could perfectly show –
How selfhood begins with a walking away,
And love is proved in the letting go.

CONDITION OR SITUATION:
The Passage of Time

PRESCRIPTION:
Oh (1990)

by Robert Creeley

Robert Creeley's poem 'Oh' meditates on the passage of time and the physical and emotional effects of aging. The poem's spare, direct language underscores a sense of vulnerability and resignation that comes with growing older. Creeley reflects on the diminishing of bodily strength and the fading of former passions, conveying an acute awareness of mortality and the inevitability of change.

Despite these losses, there is a subtle acceptance woven throughout the poem, as if the speaker is coming to terms with the limitations and realities that age brings. Through this honest portrayal, Creeley acknowledges the ache of nostalgia and the poignancy of memory, suggesting that aging involves both sorrow for what is lost and a quiet wisdom in accepting the present. The poem's message is clear: aging, though often tinged with sadness, can bring a reflective clarity and a hard-won grace.

Oh stay awhile,
sad sagging flesh
and bones gone brittle.
Stay in place,
agèd face, teeth,
don't go.
Inside and out
the flaccid change
of bodily parts,
mechanics of action,
mind's collapsing
habits, all
echo here
in mottled skin, blurred eye,
reiterated mumble.
Lift to the vacant air
some sigh, some sign
I'm still inside.

CONDITION OR SITUATION:
The Need for Basic Humanity

PRESCRIPTION:
Mediterranean Blue (2019)

by Naomi Shihab Nye

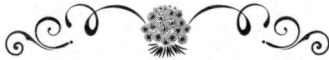

On the day I added Naomi Shihab Nye's powerful and important poem to this collection, the news was full of stories about desperate people making the perilous journey across the English Channel. Many thousands more make similarly hazardous trips across the Mediterranean's bright blue waters, fleeing famine, war and the catastrophic impact of climate change, in the hope of building a safe and happy life for themselves and their families in a different country.

I see no need to add anything else to Naomi Shihab Nye's words (herself part of a displaced family), but let them do the job for which they are intended and remind us of basic human decency and our duty to protect each other.

If you are a child of a refugee, you do not
sleep easily when they are crossing the sea
on small rafts and you know they can't swim.
My father couldn't swim either. He swam through
sorrow, though, and made it to the other side
on a ship, pitching his old clothes overboard

at landing, then tried to be happy, make a new life.
But something inside him was always paddling home,
clinging to anything that floated—a story, a food, or face.
They are the bravest people on earth right now,
don't dare look down on them. Each mind a universe
swirling as many details as yours, as much love
for a humble place. Now the shirt is torn,
the sea too wide for comfort, and nowhere
to receive a letter for a very long time.
And if we can reach out a hand, we better.

CONDITION OR SITUATION:
Contemplating Our Insignificance in the Universe

PRESCRIPTION:
Listen! (1914)

by Vladimir Mayakovsky

Anxiety induced by looking at the stars, also known as astrophobia, is an intense and irrational fear of outer space, celestial bodies or the night sky. For those with astrophobia, the vastness and mystery of the cosmos can induce panic, heart palpitations, dizziness and fear, rather than the awe and wonder often associated with stargazing. 'Listen!' by the Russian Futurist poet Vladimir Mayakovsky takes this existential angst about the endlessness of space and our insignificance in the universe and posits the question of divine interference and fear of what might happen if the stars literally went out and did not appear. He pleads with God to make sure at least one star will always shine on.

———————— ♦ ————————

Listen,
if stars are lit,
it means there is someone who needs it.
It means that someone wants them to be,
that someone deems those speckles of spit
    magnificent.
And overwrought,
in the swirls of afternoon dust,
he bursts in on God,
afraid he might be already late.
In tears,
he kisses God's sinewy hand
and begs him to guarantee
that there will definitely be a star.
He swears
he won't be able to stand
    the starless ordeal.
Later,
he wanders around, worried,
but outwardly calm.
And to someone else, he says:

'Now,
it's all right.
You are no longer afraid,
are you?'
Listen,
if stars are lit,
it means there is someone who needs it.
It means it is essential
that every evening
at least one star should ascend
over the crest of the building.

CONDITION OR SITUATION:
Accepting Your Fate

PRESCRIPTION:
An Argument (1801)

by Thomas Moore

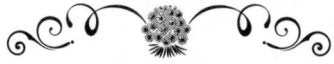

'An Argument' was written in the early 19th century and first appeared in Thomas Moore's collection *The Poetical Works of the Late Thomas Little, Esq.* when he was just twenty-two years old. One of the reasons he used the pseudonym Thomas Little was that it allowed him the freedom to examine themes of desire and morality without damaging his emerging reputation in literary circles and in London's high society.

Moore was raised as a Catholic in Ireland, and he often used his verse to challenge social and religious norms. In 'An Argument', he observes the tension between morality and instinct, playfully pointing out that, if desire and deed are equally culpable, we might as well enjoy ourselves before facing the inevitable consequences. This same theme is all too familiar in modern society, and the poem feels as relevant today as it was when the youthful poet first put pen to paper.

I've oft been told by learned friars,
That wishing and the crime are one,
And Heaven punishes desires
As much as if the deed were done.

If wishing damns us, you and I
Are damned to all our heart's content;
Come, then, at least we may enjoy
Some pleasure for our punishment!

CONDITION OR SITUATION:
Not Being Careful What You Wish for

PRESCRIPTION:
Sonnet to Liberty (1881)
by Oscar Wilde

Many a glorious revolution has not quite worked out as envisioned, leaving the impassioned participants with a degree of remorse. 'Sonnet to Liberty' by Oscar Wilde reflects on the complex nature of freedom, revolution and the cost of progress.

The poem contemplates the turbulent histories of nations that have fought for liberty, acknowledging both the bloodshed and sacrifice involved. Wilde's tone is both admiring and wary, recognizing the passionate idealism that drives people to seek freedom while also questioning the aftermath and true value of such struggles. He contrasts the fire of revolution with a personal longing for peace and an almost nostalgic connection to the stable, albeit imperfect, traditions of the past.

In the end, the sonnet expresses ambivalence toward political upheaval and proposes that while liberty is a noble pursuit, it often comes at a heavy price. Wilde's message highlights the importance of considering both the aspirations and the consequences tied to the quest for freedom.

Not that I love thy children, whose dull eyes
See nothing save their own unlovely woe,
Whose minds know nothing, nothing care to know, –
But that the roar of thy Democracies,
Thy reigns of Terror, thy great Anarchies,
Mirror my wildest passions like the sea
And give my rage a brother–! Liberty!
For this sake only do thy dissonant cries
Delight my discreet soul, else might all kings
By bloody knout or treacherous cannonades
Rob nations of their rights inviolate
And I remain unmoved – and yet, and yet,
These Christs that die upon the barricades,
God knows it I am with them, in some things.

CONDITION OR SITUATION:
Sleepless Nights Caring for a Newborn

PRESCRIPTION:
Cradle Song (1905)
by Sarojini Naidu

Sleepless nights are part and parcel of having a baby. They can take their toll, but the rewards can outweigh the bleary-eyed exhaustion and solace may be taken from this lullaby.

'Cradle Song' by Sarojini Naidu expresses the deep love, tenderness and protective instinct of a mother for her child. The poem uses soft, soothing imagery drawn from nature – such as flowers, birds and gentle breezes – to create a calming, dreamlike atmosphere meant to lull the baby to sleep. Through its melodic language and vivid descriptions, the poem highlights themes of innocence, maternal affection and the wish to shield the child from the cares and troubles of the world. The mother's voice brims with hope as she offers blessings and reassurance, dreams of happiness, and a safe space for the child to rest and grow.

Naidu's lullaby is a celebration of the purity and serenity of childhood, as well as the selfless love and comforting presence that a mother provides, making the cradle a symbol of warmth, security and boundless care.

From groves of spice,
   O'er fields of rice,
Athwart the lotus-stream,
   I bring for you,
    Aglint with dew
A little lovely dream.

   Sweet, shut your eyes,
    The wild fire-flies
Dance through the fairy neem;
   From the poppy-bole
    For you I stole
A little lovely dream.

   Dear eyes, good-night,
    In golden light
The stars around you gleam;
   On you I press
    With soft caress
A little lovely dream.

CONDITION OR SITUATION:
Shared Solitude

PRESCRIPTION:
A Lonely Moment (c.1880)
by Susan Coolidge

In 'A Lonely Moment', Susan Coolidge works through the profound ache of isolation and eventually discovers solace by recognizing the universal experience of shared solitude.

Opening in a wintry backdrop reflective of the poem's initially downbeat tone, the speaker drifts into 'dull despair' as they examine their feelings of isolation. Their thoughts wander to similar situations of solitude, like monks in their cells. But these bleak scenes take on a new meaning for the speaker as they extrapolate their personal loneliness into a universal human condition – we all yearn for company and connection.

Ultimately, the speaker's solitude is assuaged by an epiphany: even in the loneliest scenarios they can imagine, there is a 'great listening Love ... always, always heard'. For the speaker, that love is represented by divine faith, but the message of hope extends to those without religious beliefs: we may feel lonely, but we are not alone.

I sit alone in the gray,
The snow falls thick and fast,

And never a sound have I heard all day
But the wailing of the blast,
And the hiss and click of the snow, whirling to and fro.

There seems no living thing
Left in the world but I;
My thoughts fly forth on restless wing,
And drift back wearily,
Storm-beaten, buffeted, hopeless, and almost dead.

No one there is to care;
Not one to even know
Of the lonely day and the dull despair
As the hours ebb and flow,
Slow lingering, as fain to lengthen out my pain.

And I think of the monks of old,
Each in his separate cell,
Hearing no sound, except when tolled
The stated convent bell.
How could they live and bear that silence everywhere?

And I think of tumbling seas,
'Neath cruel, lonely skies;
And shipwrecked sailors over these
Stretching their hungry eyes,–
Eyes dimmed with wasting tears for weary years on years,–

Pacing the hopeless sand,
Wistful and wan and pale,

Each foam-flash like a beckoning hand,
Each wave a glancing sail,
And so for days and days, and still the sail delays.

I hide my eyes in vain,
In vain I try to smile;
That urging vision comes again,
The sailor on his isle,
With none to hear his cry, to help him live—or die!

And with the pang a thought
Breaks o'er me like the sun,
Of the great listening Love which caught
Those accents every one,
Nor lost one faintest word, but always, always heard.

The monk his vigil pale
Could lighten with a smile,
The sailor's courage need not fail
Upon his lonely isle;
For there, as here, by sea or land, the pitying Lord stood close at hand.

O coward heart of mine!
When storms shall beat again,
Hold firmly to this thought divine,
As anchorage in pain:
That, lonely though thou seemest to be, the Lord is near, remembering thee.

CONDITION OR SITUATION:
Survivor's Guilt

PRESCRIPTION:
Spared (2001)
by Wendy Cope

Written in response to the September 11, 2001 terrorist attacks in New York, 'Spared' by Wendy Cope explores themes of survivor's guilt, random chance and the fragility of human life. She contemplates how ordinary decisions and mundane moments can unexpectedly become the difference between life and death.

The poem focuses on the poet's recognition that she was safely at home watching these tragic events unfold on television, while others lost their lives simply because they were in the wrong place at the wrong time. Through simple, direct language, Cope captures the complex emotions of those who were 'spared' from tragedy: relief mixed with guilt, gratitude tangled with grief.

Cope muses how arbitrary fate can be, and how surviving a catastrophe, while others didn't, can leave us questioning our good fortune at the same time as experiencing a renewed appreciation of just how precious life is.

'That Love is all there is,
Is all we know of Love...'
Emily Dickinson

It wasn't you, it wasn't me,
Up there, two thousand feet above
A New York street. We're safe and free,
A little while, to live and love,

Imagining what might have been—
The phone-call from the blazing tower,
A last farewell on the machine,
While someone sleeps another hour,

Or worse, perhaps, to say goodbye
And listen to each other's pain,
Send helpless love across the sky,
Knowing we'll never meet again,

Or jump together, hand in hand,
To certain death. Spared all of this
For now, how well I understand
That love is all, is all there is.

CONDITION OR SITUATION:
Feeling Guilt at the Suffering of Other People

PRESCRIPTION:
The Owl (1917)
by Edward Thomas

Edward Thomas wrote 'The Owl' while serving as a soldier in World War I. The poem captures the moral unease that accompanied moments of comfort and relief during this period.

The speaker is humble from the opening stanza, framing their suffering within the wider context of a war: 'I came, hungry, and yet not starved; Cold, yet had heat within me'. Upon finding warmth, food and shelter, the speaker's peace is perforated by the owl's 'most melancholy cry', a painful reminder of those 'unable to rejoice'. Thomas was known for his understated, meditative verse, and for his use of the natural world to represent human consciousness – the owl's cry pierces the night just as the speaker's feelings of guilt cut through their moment of comfort. Thomas reminds us that we can accept comfort during times of collective hardship, but that it carries the quiet weight of guilt and awareness of others' suffering.

Downhill I came, hungry, and yet not starved;
    Cold, yet had heat within me that was proof
    Against the North wind; tired, yet so that rest
    Had seemed the sweetest thing under a roof.

Then at the inn I had food, fire, and rest,
    Knowing how hungry, cold, and tired was I.
    All of the night was quite barred out except
    An owl's cry, a most melancholy cry

Shaken out long and clear upon the hill,
    No merry note, nor cause of merriment,
    But one telling me plain what I escaped
    And others could not, that night, as in I went.

And salted was my food, and my repose,
    Salted and sobered, too, by the bird's voice
    Speaking for all who lay under the stars,
    Soldiers and poor, unable to rejoice.

CONDITION OR SITUATION:
Guilty Pleasures

PRESCRIPTION:
Doing, a Filthy Pleasure Is, and Short (c.1640)
by Ben Jonson

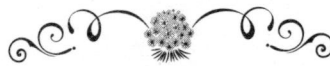

Instant gratification, although satisfying in the moment, can nonetheless leave one lamenting a guilty pleasure. Ben Jonson's 'Doing, a Filthy Pleasure Is, and Short' is a translation of a fragment from Roman courtier and author Gaius Petronius that addresses the clear dichotomy between two types of pleasure: one fleeting and base, associated with lustful actions, and the other lasting and refined, linked to loving intimacy.

On the one hand, the poet condemns the actions of 'lustful beasts' with their impulsive and animalistic pursuits and desires. In contrast, on the other hand, the poet champions a love characterized by tenderness ('closely lie and kiss'). This love is presented as sustainable and fulfilling, free from the shame and decay associated with lustful encounters.

Doing, a filthy pleasure is, and short;
And done, we straight repent us of the sport:
Let us not then rush blindly on unto it,

Like lustful beasts, that only know to do it:
For lust will languish, and that heat decay,
But thus, thus, keeping endless holiday,
Let us together closely lie and kiss,
There is no labour, nor no shame in this;
This hath pleased, doth please, and long will please; never
Can this decay, but is beginning ever.

CONDITION OR SITUATION:
Colonialism and Tourism

PRESCRIPTION:
Price We Pay for the Sun (1984)

by Grace Nichols

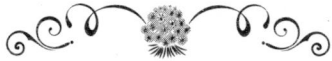

This poem explores the complex relationship between Caribbean identity, colonialism and tourism. It examines how tropical paradise comes at a cost for local inhabitants, who must serve the needs of wealthy tourists while dealing with economic inequality and cultural exploitation.

The poem highlights the irony of how Caribbean people maintain the illusion of paradise for visitors while experiencing the hardships of economic dependence and servitude. Through vivid imagery and direct language, Nichols criticizes the modern form of colonialism represented by tourism, where local culture and resources are commodified for foreign consumption.

The central message emphasizes the hidden costs of tourism in the Caribbean, questioning who truly benefits from this sun-drenched idyll and exposing the ongoing power dynamics between tourists and locals.

These islands
not picture postcards
for unravelling tourist
you know
these islands real
more real
than flesh and blood
past stone
past foam
these islands split
bone

my mother's breasts
like sleeping volcanoes
who know
what kinda sulph-furious
cancer tricking her
below
while the wind

constantly whipping
my father's tears
to salty hurricanes
and my grandmother's croon
sifting sand
water mirroring palm

CONDITION OR SITUATION:
Differing Perspectives

PRESCRIPTION:
You're Beautiful (2005)

by Simon Armitage

The unfathomable and sometimes infuriating different perspectives that exist between couples, often exacerbated by societal expectations, are satirized by Simon Armitage in his lightly sardonic poem 'You're Beautiful'.

The resolutely masculine poetic voice lists a series of stark and often slyly funny contrasts between the lives and values of two people, by implication a masculine and feminine perspective, following the mantra that 'You're Beautiful because ...' and a response of 'I'm ugly because ...' It is unclear whether these confessions of so-called ugliness are the result of anything more than humorous self-deprecation as opposed to genuine expressions of self-knowledge, but perhaps beneath the faux mockery lies an important point about tolerance of other people's habits, foibles and eccentricities.

◆

because you're classically trained.
I'm ugly because I associate piano wire with strangulation.

You're beautiful because you stop to read the cards in
   newsagents' windows about lost cats and missing dogs.
I'm ugly because of what I did to that jellyfish with a lolly-stick
   and a big stone.

You're beautiful because for you, politeness is instinctive, not
   a marketing campaign.
I'm ugly because desperation is impossible to hide.

Ugly like he is,
Beautiful like hers,
Beautiful like Venus,
Ugly like his,
Beautiful like she is,
Ugly like Mars.

You're beautiful because you believe in coincidence and the
   power of thought.
I'm ugly because I proved God to be a mathematical
   impossibility.

You're beautiful because you prefer home-made soup to the
  packet stuff.
I'm ugly because once, at a dinner party, I defended the
  aristocracy and wasn't even drunk.

You're beautiful because you can't work the remote control.
I'm ugly because of satellite television and twenty-four-hour
  rolling news.

Ugly like he is,
Beautiful like hers,
Beautiful like Venus,
Ugly like his,
Beautiful like she is,
Ugly like Mars.

You're beautiful because you cry at weddings as well as
  funerals.
I'm ugly because I think of children as another species from
  a different world.

You're beautiful because you look great in any colour
  including red.
I'm ugly because I think shopping is strictly for the acquisition
  of material goods.

You're beautiful because when you were born, undiscovered
  planets lined up to peep over the rim of your cradle and
  lay gifts of gravity and light at your miniature feet.

I'm ugly for saying 'love at first sight' is another form
   of mistaken identity, and that the most human of all
   responses is to gloat.

Ugly like he is,
Beautiful like hers,
Beautiful like Venus,
Ugly like his,
Beautiful like she is,
Ugly like Mars.

You're beautiful because you've never seen the inside of
   a car-wash.
I'm ugly because I always ask for a receipt.

You're beautiful for sending a box of shoes to the
   third world.
I'm ugly because I remember the telephone of ex-girlfriends
   and the year Schubert was born.

You're beautiful because you sponsored a parrot in a zoo.
I'm ugly because when I sigh it's like the slow collapse
   of a circus tent

Ugly like he is,
Beautiful like hers,
Beautiful like Venus,
Ugly like his,
Beautiful like she is,
Ugly like Mars.

You're beautiful because you can point at a man in a uniform and laugh.
I'm ugly because I was a police informer in a previous life.

You're beautiful because you drink a litre of water and eat three pieces of fruit a day.
I'm ugly for taking the line that a meal without meat is a beautiful woman with one eye.

You're beautiful because you don't see love as a competition and you know how to lose.
I'm ugly because I kissed the FA Cup and then held it up to the crowd.

You're beautiful because of a single buttercup in the top buttonhole of your cardigan.
I'm ugly because I said the World's Strongest Woman was a muscleman in a dress.

You're beautiful because you couldn't live in a lighthouse.
I'm ugly for making hand-shadows in front of the giant bulb, so when they look up, the captains of vessels in distress see the ears of a rabbit, or the eye of a fox, or the legs of a galloping black horse.

Ugly like he is,
Beautiful like hers,
Beautiful like Venus,
Ugly like his,
Beautiful like she is,

Ugly like Mars.
Ugly like he is,
Beautiful like hers,
Beautiful like Venus,
Ugly like his,
Beautiful like she is,
Ugly like Mars.

CONDITION OR SITUATION:
A Hollow Liaison

PRESCRIPTION:
Party Piece (1967)

by Brian Patten

Brian Patten's 'Party Piece' explores the hollowness of meaningless sex and one-night stands. Two people, left at a party after all the guests have gone home, have meaningless, loveless (probably drunken) sex.

It is a disquieting poem: the almost coercive insistence of the male voice, that the participants should 'unclip our minds' – not think about it too much, but just follow the urge to indulge 'the mad, mangled crocodile of love' – sets up the sad irony of the final lines. In the end, with some choice details ('woodbines', 'Guinness stains'), Patten evokes the seediness of the encounter and the emptiness felt by the participants afterwards. A cautionary tale for anyone tempted into a meaningless one-night stand.

He said:

'Let's stay here
Now this place has emptied
And make gentle pornography with one another,
While the partygoers go out
And the dawn creeps in,
Like a stranger.

Let us not hesitate
Over what we know
Or over how cold this place has become,
But let's unclip our minds
And let tumble free
The mad, mangled crocodile of love.'

So they did,
There among the woodbines and Guinness stains,
And later he caught a bus and she a train
And all there was between them then
was rain.

5

Remedies for Everyday Living

CONDITION OR SITUATION:
Coping with All That Life Can Throw at You

PRESCRIPTION:
If (1910)

by Rudyard Kipling

Sometimes life just seems to get at us at every turn, and each waking moment can seem like a struggle against multiple life issues and adversities. Routinely voted 'The Nation's Favourite Poem' in the UK, 'If' by Rudyard Kipling is tribute to the good-old-fashioned British 'stiff upper lip'.

Kipling proposes that the way to best navigate life's choppy waters is to retain self-control and a sense of calm, reason, self-discipline and perseverance in the face of challenges and misfortune. The poem takes the form of a father imparting words of wisdom to his son, and the 'stand up and be a man' masculinity is very much of its time (the poem was originally written in 1895, although not published until 1910). But within this message are several principles of the stoic philosophy of Marcus Aurelius, of whom Kipling was an admirer.

If you can keep your head when all about you
    Are losing theirs and blaming it on you;

If you can trust yourself when all men doubt you,
    But make allowance for their doubting too;
If you can wait and not be tired by waiting,
    Or being lied about, don't deal in lies,
Or being hated don't give way to hating,
    And yet don't look too good, nor talk too wise;

If you can dream – and not make dreams your master;
    If you can think – and not make thoughts your aim,
If you can meet with Triumph and Disaster
    And treat those two impostors just the same;
If you can bear to hear the truth you've spoken
    Twisted by knaves to make a trap for fools,
Or watch the things you gave your life to, broken,
    And stoop and build 'em up with worn-out tools;

If you can make one heap of all your winnings
    And risk it on one turn of pitch-and-toss,
And lose, and start again at your beginnings
    And never breathe a word about your loss;
If you can force your heart and nerve and sinew
    To serve your turn long after they are gone,
And so hold on when there is nothing in you
    Except the Will which says to them: 'Hold on!'

If you can talk with crowds and keep your virtue,
    Or walk with Kings – nor lose the common touch,
If neither foes nor loving friends can hurt you,
    If all men count with you, but none too much;

If you can fill the unforgiving minute
   With sixty seconds' worth of distance run,
Yours is the Earth and everything that's in it,
   And – which is more – you'll be a Man, my son!

CONDITION OR SITUATION:
Challenging Attitudes to Diversity, Difference and Prejudice

PRESCRIPTION:
Diversity in de Market
(calypso poem) (2022)
by John Agard

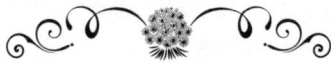

This piece by Guyanese-born British poet John Agard is a celebration of the richness of mixed heritage and multiculturalism, illustrating that it is not a flaw but a source of strength. Agard came to the UK in 1977 at a time when cultural norms in Britain were constantly being questioned. Difference was often viewed with suspicion and distrust. He uses the imagery of a marketplace with its many different goods peacefully co-existing to highlight society's potential – all are welcome, no segregation here, only 'harmonious cohabitation'.

Written in free verse in a mix of English and Creole, with a calypso swing, 'Diversity in de Market' sits comfortably in the tradition of spoken – even sung – poetry: words are shared and enjoyed together – in a community. In this way the poem reflects the dynamic vibrancy of the marketplace itself, where ideas and information are exchanged verbally, encouraging unity and community, rather than hostility and separation.

(spoken)
To learn how dis ting diversity does operate
I went by Brixton market to investigate,
how de fruit and veg dem does integrate.
Ah saw Apple and Mango conversing cosily
Ripe Plantain had no quarrel with Broccoli.
Aubergine don't bear grudge 'gainst Piri-Piri.
I was impressed how Pineapple spoke sweetly
and when Red Pepper responded discreetly
I knew de fruit and veg dem could teach a nation
de secret of harmonious cohabitation.
So if you want learn 'bout dis ting diversity,
observe Butternut Squash and de little Lychee

(sung, calypso tempo)
In de fruit and veg market it was plain to see
de red yellow purple green live in harmony.
Yes, fruit and veg dem show each other respect,
no, Cucumber never raise a finger to Courgette,
no, Cucumber never raise a finger to Courgette

(spoken)
Then I saw Saltfish chatting up Chorizo
like de two o' dem does talk de same lingo.
Gammon and Mackerel held no grievance.
Black Pudding and Salami struck up alliance.
So if you want learn 'bout social etiquette
just study de ways of Oxtail Veal Brisket

(sung, calypso tempo)
In de fish and meat market too it was plain to see
de black white pink brown also live in harmony.
Yes, fish and meat dem show each other respect,
no, Ah never see a fight between two fillet yet,
man, Ah never see a fight between two fillet yet.

CONDITION OR SITUATION:
Struggling with Life Choices

PRESCRIPTION:
The Road Not Taken (1915)

by Robert Frost

There are many moments in life when we are faced with difficult choices to make and genuine dilemmas. 'The

Road Not Taken' by Robert Frost explores the themes of choice, regret and the illusion of a unique life path. The poet recounts a moment where they chose one of two equally worn paths, later framing that decision as the one that 'made all the difference'.

However, the poem also reveals the poet's awareness that the roads were equally worn, suggesting the choice was not really quite so momentous. This highlights the human tendency to romanticize and overemphasize the importance of certain decisions, perhaps to cope with the possible regrets of the paths not taken.

Two roads diverged in a yellow wood,
And sorry I could not travel both
And be one traveler, long I stood
And looked down one as far as I could
To where it bent in the undergrowth;

Then took the other, as just as fair,
And having perhaps the better claim,
Because it was grassy and wanted wear;
Though as for that the passing there
Had worn them really about the same,

And both that morning equally lay
In leaves no step had trodden black.
Oh, I kept the first for another day!
Yet knowing how way leads on to way,
I doubted if I should ever come back.

I shall be telling this with a sigh
Somewhere ages and ages hence:
Two roads diverged in a wood, and I—
I took the one less traveled by,
And that has made all the difference.

CONDITION OR SITUATION:
Feeling Smothered by Urban Living

PRESCRIPTION:
The Lake Isle of Innisfree (1890)

by William Butler Yeats

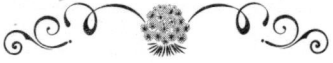

'The Lake Isle of Innisfree's central theme revolves around the poet's desire to leave the city and live a life immersed in nature. Innisfree is presented as an idyllic place where he can find peace and solitude. The poem contrasts the speaker's life in the city with the peaceful, natural existence he envisions on Innisfree. The city is depicted as 'grey' and unnatural, while Innisfree is a place of 'purple glow', 'bee-loud glade' and the sounds of nature. Yeats suggests that a return to nature offers unique spiritual rewards, allowing him to connect with his inner self and find peace of mind.

'The Lake Isle of Innisfree' reflects Yeats' own deep connection to the Irish landscape and his desire for a more rural lifestyle. It also resonates with readers seeking a connection to nature and a desire for a simpler life.

I will arise and go now, and go to Innisfree,
And a small cabin build there, of clay and wattles made:
Nine bean rows will I have there, a hive for the honey bee,
And live alone in the bee-loud glade.

And I shall have some peace there, for peace comes dropping slow,
Dropping from the veils of the morning to where the cricket sings;
There midnight's all a glimmer, and noon a purple glow,
And evening full of the linnet's wings.

I will arise and go now, for always night and day
I hear lake water lapping with low sounds by the shore;
While I stand on the roadway, or on the pavements gray,
I hear it in the deep heart's core.

CONDITION OR SITUATION:
Risk Aversion

PRESCRIPTION:
Roll the Dice (1997)
by Charles Bukowski

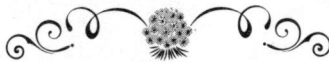

'Fools rush in where angels fear to tread,' sang Elvis Presley, borrowing a sentiment from Alexander Pope. Not so Charles Bukowski, who saw nobility in embracing risk. Bukowski's 'Roll the Dice' champions total commitment to one's passion or calling. The poem serves as a raw, unflinching manifesto for wholehearted dedication, arguing that anything pursued must be done with complete abandon – go all the way or not at all. Bukowski suggests that true fulfilment comes only through risking everything for what matters most to you, even when facing isolation, doubt and potential ruin.

The work condemns half-measures and compromise, presenting a stark choice between mediocre safety and meaningful struggle. It embraces the inherent suffering that accompanies authentic living while promising that such devotion ultimately brings a transcendent sense of purpose. In essence, Bukowski challenges readers to gamble everything on their deepest convictions, finding liberation in total commitment.

if you're going to try, go all the
way.
otherwise, don't even start.

if you're going to try, go all the
way. this could mean losing girlfriends,
wives, relatives, jobs and
maybe your mind.

go all the way.
it could mean not eating for 3 or
4 days.
it could mean freezing on a
park bench.
it could mean jail,
it could mean derision,
mockery,
isolation.
isolation is the gift,
all the others are a test of your
endurance, of
how much you really want to
do it.
and you'll do it
despite rejection and the
worst odds
and it will be better than
anything else
you can imagine.

if you're going to try,
go all the way.
there is no other feeling like
that.
you will be alone with the
gods
and the nights will flame with
fire.

do it, do it, do it.
do it.

all the way
all the way.
you will ride life straight to
perfect laughter,
it's the only good fight
there is.

CONDITION OR SITUATION:
The Horrors of Corporate Culture

PRESCRIPTION:
Executive (1974)

by John Betjeman

'Executive' by John Betjeman is a satirical poem that criticizes the superficiality and materialism of modern business culture, particularly focusing on the emerging executive class in post-war Britain.

The poem mocks the pretentiousness and artificial lifestyle of a young business executive, highlighting his obsession with status symbols and modern conveniences. Through details about the executive's possessions, home and lifestyle choices, Betjeman paints a picture of someone more concerned with appearing successful than having genuine substance.

Key themes include materialism, social climbing and the erosion of traditional values in favour of modern consumerism. The poem criticizes the standardization of middle-class life and the emphasis on superficial markers of success.

The overall message is a critique of the shallow values of modern corporate capitalism and the way people sacrifice authenticity for the appearance of success. Betjeman uses irony and satire to expose the emptiness behind the executive's seemingly enviable lifestyle.

I am a young executive. No cuffs than mine are cleaner;
I have a Slimline brief-case and I use the firm's Cortina.
In every roadside hostelry from here to Burgess Hill
The maîtres d'hôtel all know me well, and let me sign the bill.

You ask me what it is I do. Well, actually, you know,
I'm partly a liaison man, and partly P. R. O.
Essentially, I integrate the current export drive
And basically I'm viable from ten o'clock till five.

For vital off-the-record work – that's talking transport-wise –
I've a scarlet Aston-Martin – and does she go? She flies!
Pedestrians and dogs and cats, we mark them down for slaughter.
I also own a speedboat which has never touched the water.

She's built of fibre-glass, of course. I call her 'Mandy Jane'
After a bird I used to know – No soda, please, just plain –
And how did I acquire her? Well, to tell you about that
And to put you in the picture, I must wear my other hat.

I do some mild developing. The sort of place I need
Is a quiet country market town that's rather run to seed
A luncheon and a drink or two, a little savoir faire –
I fix the Planning Officer, the Town Clerk and the Mayor.

And if some Preservationist attempts to interfere
A 'dangerous structure' notice from the Borough Engineer
Will settle any buildings that are standing in our way –
The modern style, sir, with respect, has really come to stay.

CONDITION OR SITUATION:
Questioning the Nature of Reality

PRESCRIPTION:
A Dream Within a Dream (1849)
by Edgar Allan Poe

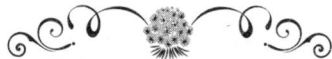

'A Dream Within a Dream' by Edgar Allan Poe explores the elusive nature of reality and the transient quality of human existence. The poem expresses deep uncertainty about whether life itself is merely an illusion, comparing existence to grains of sand slipping through one's fingers. Through its two stanzas, the speaker grapples with loss, time's relentless passage and the inability to hold on to anything permanent in life.

Poe questions whether everything we perceive as real might actually be part of an elaborate dream, suggesting that the distinction between reality and fantasy may be meaningless. The imagery of golden sand being taken by the ocean waves symbolizes how time and fate inevitably carry away our hopes, loves and certainties. The poem's ultimate message conveys the haunting possibility that all human experience – our relationships, achievements and understanding of reality – might be as insubstantial and fleeting as a dream.

Take this kiss upon the brow!
And, in parting from you now,
Thus much let me avow—
You are not wrong, who deem
That my days have been a dream;
Yet if hope has flown away
In a night, or in a day,
In a vision, or in none,
Is it therefore the less *gone*?
All that we see or seem
Is but a dream within a dream.

I stand amid the roar
Of a surf-tormented shore,
And I hold within my hand
Grains of the golden sand—
How few! yet how they creep
Through my fingers to the deep,
While I weep—while I weep!
O God! can I not grasp
Them with a tighter clasp?
O God! can I not save
One from the pitiless wave?
Is *all* that we see or seem
But a dream within a dream?

CONDITION OR SITUATION:
Feeling Lonely at Night

PRESCRIPTION:
At That Hour (1907)
by James Joyce

James Joyce's delicate poem captures a moment of profound stillness and contemplation as day transitions to night. Through a series of intimate questions posed to an absent beloved, the poem explores the spiritual connection between separated lovers, suggesting that true emotional bonds transcend physical distance. Joyce weaves natural imagery, such as the night wind and approaching sunrise, with musical metaphors and expressions of longing to create a dreamlike atmosphere where memory and present experience blur together. The repeated phrase 'when all things have repose' establishes a meditative state where the speaker reaches toward their distant lover.

The poem ultimately reflects on how shared moments of beauty and tenderness persist in memory, creating a bittersweet communion across time and space, where love exists in quiet moments of reflection.

At that hour when all things have repose,
O lonely watcher of the skies,
Do you hear the night wind and the sighs

Of harps playing unto Love to unclose
The pale gates of sunrise?

When all things repose, do you alone
Awake to hear the sweet harps play
To Love before him on his way,
And the night wind answering in antiphon
Till night is overgone?

Play on, invisible harps, unto Love,
Whose way in heaven is aglow
At that hour when soft lights come and go,
Soft sweet music in the air above
And in the earth below.

CONDITION OR SITUATION:
Building Resilience

PRESCRIPTION:
Life (1846)

by Charlotte Brontë

'Life' centres on the theme of resilience in the face of life's hardships and the human capacity to endure difficult circumstances. The poem portrays life as a constant struggle, yet emphasizes the importance of maintaining hope and determination. Charlotte Brontë suggests that, while we cannot control the challenges life presents, we can control our response to them.

The poem's message is deeply stoic, encouraging readers to face adversity with courage rather than seeking escape or giving in to despair. Through vivid weather imagery contrasted with moments of calm, Brontë conveys the idea that both suffering and peace are temporary states.

The main message is one of perseverance: though life may be difficult, we must continue to fight and stay strong, as better days will eventually come.

Life, believe, is not a dream
So dark as sages say;
Oft a little morning rain
Foretells a pleasant day.
Sometimes there are clouds of gloom,
But these are transient all;
If the shower will make the roses bloom,
O why lament its fall ?
Rapidly, merrily,
Life's sunny hours flit by,
Gratefully, cheerily
Enjoy them as they fly!
What though Death at times steps in,
And calls our Best away?
What though sorrow seems to win,

O'er hope, a heavy sway?
Yet Hope again elastic springs,
Unconquered, though she fell;
Still buoyant are her golden wings,
Still strong to bear us well.
Manfully, fearlessly,
The day of trial bear,
For gloriously, victoriously,
Can courage quell despair!

CONDITION OR SITUATION:
Being Drunk

PRESCRIPTION:
Intoxication (1864)
by Charles Baudelaire

Charles Baudelaire's 'Intoxication' is a passionate call to embrace inebriation, not merely through alcohol, but any way that elevates one above the mundane reality of everyday life. The poem advocates a metaphorical and literal drunkenness: 'With wine, with poetry, with virtue', or whatever medium helps escape the crushing weight of time and conventional existence. Baudelaire suggests that sobriety equals submission to time, responsibility and memory – elements that he views as oppressive forces.

The poem's message is fundamentally about seeking transcendence and intense living, encouraging readers to break free from the ordinary and find their own path to euphoria. It's both a rebellion against societal norms and a prescription for dealing with life's hardships through the pursuit of ecstatic experiences.

One must be for ever drunken: that is the sole question of importance. If you would not feel the horrible burden of Time that bruises your shoulders and bends you to the earth, you must be drunken without cease. But how? With wine, with poetry, with virtue, with what you please. But be drunken. And if sometimes, on the steps of a palace, on the green grass by a moat, or in the dull loneliness of your chamber, you should waken up, your intoxication already lessened or gone, ask of the wind, of the wave, of the star, of the bird, of the timepiece; ask of all that flees, all that sighs, all that revolves, all that sings, all that speaks, ask of these the hour; and wind and wave and star and bird and timepiece will answer you:

'It is the hour to be drunken! Lest you be the martyred slaves of Time, intoxicate yourselves, be drunken without cease! With wine, with poetry, with virtue, or with what you will.'

CONDITION OR SITUATION:
Dealing with Life's Deceptions

PRESCRIPTION:
Consolation (1825)
by Alexander Pushkin

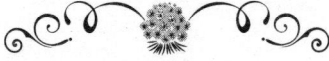

'Consolation', often called 'If by Life You Were Deceived', by Russian poet Alexander Pushkin explores themes of resilience, hope and the cyclical nature of life's disappointments and joys. The poem offers consolation and wisdom to those who have experienced betrayal or disillusionment, suggesting that while pain and deception are inevitable parts of life, they are also temporary. Pushkin advocates for maintaining optimism despite life's setbacks, encouraging readers not to become bitter or withdrawn after experiencing disappointment. The poem emphasizes the importance of remaining open to future possibilities and maintaining faith in better days ahead, even when current circumstances seem bleak.

Through its gentle, advisory tone, Pushkin argues that emotional healing comes through accepting life's deceptions while still preserving hope for tomorrow. The overall theme promotes emotional resilience and the wisdom of maintaining a balanced perspective that neither dwells in past hurts nor closes oneself off from future joys.

Life,—does it disappoint thee?
Grieve not, nor be angry thou!
In days of sorrow gentle be:
Come shall, believe, the joyful day.

In the future lives the heart:
Is the present sad indeed?
'T is but a moment, all will pass;
Once in the past, it shall be dear.

CONDITION OR SITUATION:
The Horrors of Materialism and Modernity

PRESCRIPTION:
The World Is Too Much with Us (1807)
by William Wordsworth

'The World Is Too Much with Us' is a powerful critique of society's growing disconnect from nature in favour of materialistic pursuits. Written as a Petrarchan sonnet (comprised of an octave of eight lines posing a problem, followed by a sestet of six lines that provide a resolution or reflection), the poem laments humanity's loss of spiritual and emotional connection to the natural world during the Industrial Revolution.

Wordsworth argues that people have become too preoccupied with 'getting and spending', sacrificing their fundamental relationship with nature's beauty and power. He depicts nature through vivid imagery of the sea, winds and flowers, contrasting these eternal elements with humanity's superficial concerns. The poet expresses profound regret that humans have become desensitized to nature's majesty, suggesting we have 'given our hearts away'.

The poem's message emphasizes that by prioritizing material wealth and progress, society has lost something essential to the human spirit. Wordsworth suggests that reconnecting with nature is crucial for spiritual fulfilment, even expressing a wish to return to pagan times when people felt more intimately connected to natural forces.

The world is too much with us; late and soon,
Getting and spending we lay waste our powers;
Little we see in nature that is ours;
We have given our hearts away, a sordid boon!
This Sea that bares her bosom to the moon;
The Winds that will be howling at all hours
And are up-gathered now like sleeping flowers;
For this, for every thing, we are out of tune;
It moves us not—Great God! I'd rather be
A Pagan suckled in a creed outworn;

So might I, standing on this pleasant lea,
Have glimpses that would make me less forlorn;
Have sight of Proteus coming from the sea;
Or hear old Triton blow his wreathed horn.

CONDITION OR SITUATION:
Ingrained Racism

PRESCRIPTION:
Telephone Conversation (1963)

by Wole Soyinka

'Telephone Conversation' by Wole Soyinka examines themes of racism, prejudice and social hypocrisy through the perspective of a Black man seeking to rent an apartment. When the landlady enquires about his skin colour, the conversation exposes the absurdity and cruelty of racial discrimination. Through irony, wit and stark dialogue, Soyinka highlights how deeply ingrained racism disrupts ordinary human interactions and strips individuals of their dignity. The poem's message is a sharp critique of societal biases, illustrating how racist attitudes persist even in seemingly mundane situations. Ultimately, Soyinka calls attention to the need for honest self-examination and the dismantling of prejudice in order to create truly equitable relationships between people.

The price seemed reasonable, location
Indifferent. The landlady swore she lived
Off premises. Nothing remained
But self-confession. 'Madam,' I warned,
'I hate a wasted journey – I am African.'
Silence. Silenced transmission of pressurized good-breeding
Voice, when it came,
Lipstick coated, long gold-rolled
Cigarette-holder pipped. Caught I was, foully.
'HOW DARK?'... I had not misheard ... 'ARE YOU LIGHT OR
VERY DARK?' Button B. Button A. Stench
Of rancid breath of public hide-and-speak.
Red booth. Red pillar-box. Red double-tiered
Omnibus squelching tar.
It was real! Shamed
By ill-mannered silence, surrender
Pushed dumbfoundment to beg simplification.
Considerate she was, varying the emphasis –
'ARE YOU DARK? OR VERY LIGHT?' Revelation came.
'You mean – like plain or milk chocolate?'
Her accent was clinical, crushing in its light
Impersonality. Rapidly, wave-length adjusted
I chose. 'West African sepia' – and as afterthought,
'Down in my passport.' Silence for spectroscopic

Flight of fancy, till truthfulness changed her accent
Hard on the mouthpiece 'WHAT'S THAT?' conceding 'DON'T
KNOW WHAT THAT IS.' 'Like brunette.'
'THAT'S DARK, ISN'T IT?'
'Not altogether.
Facially, I am brunette, but madam you should see the rest of
me. Palm of my hand, soles of my feet.
Are a peroxide blonde. Friction, caused –
Foolishly madam – by sitting down, has turned
My bottom raven black – One moment madam!' – sensing
Her receiver rearing on the thunderclap
About my ears – 'Madam,' I pleaded, 'wouldn't you rather
See for yourself?'

CONDITION OR SITUATION:
Acceptance of Change

PRESCRIPTION:
To Autumn (1820)

by John Keats

It's hard to move on sometimes, and the old adage that a change is as good as a rest doesn't always resonate with people, content as they are for things to stay the same. 'To

Autumn' by John Keats is a rich meditation on the beauty and ephemerality of the autumn season. The poem explores themes of nature's abundance, the passage of time, and the inevitability of change.

Keats vividly describes the fullness and maturity of autumn, emphasizing how it is both the culmination of growth and a prelude to decline. While the poem revels in the sensory pleasures of the harvest, it also acknowledges the quiet approach of winter, suggesting a gentle acceptance of life's cycles and endings. The overall message invites readers to find beauty and contentment in each moment, appreciating the richness of the present even as it inevitably fades. Through this celebration of autumn's splendour and quiet melancholy, Keats affirms the value of accepting the transience of all things, the nature of change and the progression of life.

Season of mists and mellow fruitfulness,
   Close bosom-friend of the maturing sun;
Conspiring with him how to load and bless
   With fruit the vines that round the thatch-eves run;
To bend with apples the moss'd cottage-trees,
   And fill all fruit with ripeness to the core;
      To swell the gourd, and plump the hazel shells
   With a sweet kernel; to set budding more,
And still more, later flowers for the bees,
Until they think warm days will never cease,
      For Summer has o'er-brimm'd their clammy cells.

Who hath not seen thee oft amid thy store?
   Sometimes whoever seeks abroad may find
Thee sitting careless on a granary floor,
   Thy hair soft-lifted by the winnowing wind;
Or on a half-reap'd furrow sound asleep,
   Drows'd with the fume of poppies, while thy hook
      Spares the next swath and all its twined flowers:
And sometimes like a gleaner thou dost keep
   Steady thy laden head across a brook;
   Or by a cyder-press, with patient look,
      Thou watchest the last oozings hours by hours.

Where are the songs of Spring? Ay, where are they?
   Think not of them, thou hast thy music too,—
While barred clouds bloom the soft-dying day,
   And touch the stubble-plains with rosy hue;
Then in a wailful choir the small gnats mourn
   Among the river sallows, borne aloft
      Or sinking as the light wind lives or dies;
And full-grown lambs loud bleat from hilly bourn;
   Hedge-crickets sing; and now with treble soft
   The red-breast whistles from a garden-croft;
      And gathering swallows twitter in the skies.

CONDITION OR SITUATION:
Shattered Dreams

PRESCRIPTION:
La Bodega Sold Dreams (1980)

by Miguel Piñero

'La Bodega Sold Dreams' vividly portrays the struggles and hopes of urban life within a marginalized community. The poem centres on the bodega as a symbol of both survival and lost aspirations, where dreams are bought and sold against the harsh realities of poverty, addiction and disenfranchisement.

Miguel Piñero explores themes of resilience, cultural identity and the complex relationship between hope and despair through stark imagery, revealing how people seek connection and meaning in a world often marked by hardship and disappointment.

The poem emphasizes humanity's persistence and the power of dreams amid adversity, while also mourning how systemic forces suppress these hopes.

---

dreamt i was a poet
&
writin' silver sailin' songs

words
strong & powerful crashing thru
walls of steel & concrete
erected in minds weak
&
those asleep
replacin' a hobby of paper candy
wrappin', collectin'
potent to pregnate sterile young
thoughts

i dreamt i was this poeta
words glitterin' brite & bold
strikin' a new rush for gold
in las bodegas
where our poets' words & songs
are sung
but
sunlite stealin' thru venetian
blinds
eyes hatin', workin' of time
clock
sweatin'
&
swearin'
&
slavin'
for the final dime
runnin' a maze
a token ride

perspiration insultin' poets
pride
words stoppin' on red
goin' on green
poets' dreams
endin' in a factoria as one
in a million
unseen
buyin' bodega sold dreams …

CONDITION OR SITUATION:
The Excesses of Capitalism

PRESCRIPTION:
Velocity of Money (1986)

by Allen Ginsberg

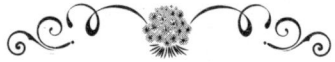

'Velocity of Money' by Allen Ginsberg is a scathing critique of capitalism and modern American society's obsession with wealth and consumption. The poem uses sarcasm and irony to explore how money circulates through society at an increasingly frantic pace, destroying human relationships and leaving spiritual values abandoned in its wake.

Ginsberg portrays money as a destructive force that transforms everything it touches into a commodity, including human relationships and artistic expression. The poem highlights the dehumanizing effects of capitalism, showing how the rapid movement of money creates anxiety, alienation and spiritual emptiness. Through vivid imagery and a sense of decay, Ginsberg illustrates how the endless pursuit of wealth has become a kind of modern religion, replacing genuine human connection and meaningful experience. The poem warns against the corrupting influence of capitalism and its ability to reduce human existence to mere financial transactions.

I'm delighted by the velocity of money as it whistles through the windows
of Lower East Side
Delighted by skyscrapers rising the old grungy apartments falling on
84th Street
Delighted by inflation that drives me out on the street
After all what good's the family farm, why eat turkey by thousands every
Thanksgiving?
Why not have Star Wars? Why have the same old America?!?
George Washington wasn't good enough! Tom Paine pain in the neck,
Whitman what a jerk!
I'm delighted by double digit interest rates in the Capitalist world

I always was a communist, now we'll win
an usury makes the walls thinner, books thicker & dumber
Usury makes my poetry more valuable
my manuscripts worth their weight in useless gold –
Now everybody's atheist like me, nothing's sacred
buy and sell your grandmother, eat up old age homes,
Peddle babies on the street, pretty boys for sale on Times Square –
You can shoot heroin, I can sniff cocaine,
macho men can fite on the Nicaraguan border and get paid with paper!
The velocity's what counts as the National Debt gets higher
Everybody running after the rising dollar
Crowds of joggers down broadway past City Hall on the way to the Fed
Nobody reads Dostoyevsky books so they'll have to give a passing ear
to my fragmented ravings in between President's speeches
Nothing's happening but the collapse of the Economy
so I can go back to sleep till the landlord wins his eviction suit in court.

CONDITION OR SITUATION:
Unfulfilling Days

PRESCRIPTION:
Count That Day Lost (1887)
by George Eliot

We may all feel from time to time that our days are unfulfilled, that we are just drifting through a well-worn routine almost as if we are sleepwalking through life. George Eliot has a remedy with her poem 'Count That Day Lost'. She conveys a profound message about measuring the true value of each day through acts of kindness which have a positive impact on others. The poem suggests that a day should not be judged by personal achievements or material gains, but rather by whether we've made someone else's life better. Eliot emphasizes that even small gestures, like offering a kind word or easing another's burden, make a day worthwhile.

Conversely, if we've gone through a day without helping anyone or bringing joy to others, that day should be considered 'lost'. The poem's central theme is moral responsibility, compassion and finding meaning through serving others.

If you sit down at set of sun
And count the acts that you have done,
And, counting, find

One self-denying deed, one word
That eased the heart of him who heard,
One glance most kind
That fell like sunshine where it went—
Then you may count that day well spent.

But if, through all the livelong day,
You've cheered no heart, by yea or nay —
If, through it all
You've nothing done that you can trace
That brought the sunshine to one face—
No act most small
That helped some soul and nothing cost—
Then count that day as worse than lost.

CONDITION OR SITUATION:

In Need of Inspiration in Dark Moments

PRESCRIPTION:

Desiderata (1927)

by Max Ehrmann

If ever there were a poem to live by, one that can inspire the troubled mind in life's bleakest moments, it is surely this popular prose poem. The 'Desiderata' was written in 1927 by American Max Ehrmann; sadly, he would not live to see the widespread popularity it would gain in the 1960s – nor how its gentle, timeless wisdom would continue to resonate with millions of readers around the globe to the present day.

In 'Desiderata', Ehrmann urges us to see the goodness in life, to be strong and make our way in this 'beautiful world' with serenity and kindness, remaining steadfast and calm in the face of adversity – 'in the noisy confusion of life'. So, let us follow these principles and 'Strive to be happy'.

Go placidly amid the noise and the haste,
and remember what peace there may be in silence.

As far as possible, without surrender,
be on good terms with all persons.
Speak your truth quietly and clearly;
and listen to others,
even to the dull and the ignorant;
they too have their story.

Avoid loud and aggressive persons;
they are vexatious to the spirit.

If you compare yourself with others,
you may become vain or bitter,
for always there will be greater and lesser persons than
    yourself.
Enjoy your achievements as well as your plans.

Keep interested in your own career, however humble;
it is a real possession in the changing fortunes of time.

Exercise caution in your business affairs,
for the world is full of trickery.
But let this not blind you to what virtue there is;
many persons strive for high ideals,
and everywhere life is full of heroism.
Be yourself. Especially do not feign affection.
Neither be cynical about love,
for in the face of all aridity and disenchantment,
it is as perennial as the grass.

Take kindly the counsel of the years,
gracefully surrendering the things of youth.
Nurture strength of spirit to shield you in sudden misfortune.
But do not distress yourself with dark imaginings.
Many fears are born of fatigue and loneliness.

Beyond a wholesome discipline,
be gentle with yourself.
You are a child of the universe
no less than the trees and the stars;
you have a right to be here.
And whether or not it is clear to you,
no doubt the universe is unfolding as it should.

Therefore be at peace with God,
whatever you conceive Him to be.
And whatever your labors and aspirations,

in the noisy confusion of life,
keep peace in your soul.

With all its sham, drudgery, and broken dreams,
it is still a beautiful world.
Be cheerful. Strive to be happy.

CONDITION OR SITUATION:
Learning to Live for This Day

PRESCRIPTION:
Odes 3:29
(Stanzas I–XII) (15th century)
by Horace

'Odes 3.29' was written around 23 BCE, during a period of relative political stability under Augustus. In the poem, Horace urges his friend and patron Maecenas to embrace the art of living in the present. While Maecenas remains 'intent on cares of state' in Rome, Horace warns that it's foolish to seek to know the future, as it lies 'beyond bounds to mortal minds assigned'. Everything which is not the present moment 'flows onward as the river runs' – the past is no more, and the future will arrive but is unknowable for now. Horace suggests that by accepting the passing nature of all things, we can find peace and a freedom that wealth and status cannot secure. For, happy is he who can say each day: 'I have lived'.

Long since, Maecenas sprung from Tuscan kings,
A vintage mellowing in its virgin cask,
    Balms to anoint the hair,
        And roses meet for wreaths on honoured brows,

Wait at my home for thee. Snatch leisure brief,
And turn thy gaze from Tibur's waterfalls
    The slopes of Aesula,
        And parricidal Telegon's blue hills;

Desert fastidious wealth, and that proud pile
Soaring aloft, the neighbour of the clouds;
    Cease to admire the smoke,
        The riches, and the roar of prosperous Rome.

Sweet to the wealthy the relief of change;
Nor needs it tapestried woof nor Tyrian pall
    For simple feast, whose mirth
        In humble roofs unknits the brows of Care.

Now, hidden long, Andromeda's bright sire
Glares forth revealed: now rages Procyon,
    And the mad Lion-star,
        As Sol brings back the sultry days of drought.

Now doth the shepherd, with his languid flock,
Seek streams and shades, and thickets dense, the lair
    Of the rough Forest-God;
        And silent margins miss the wandering winds.

All rest save thou, intent on cares of state
And fears lest aught against thy Rome be planned
    In farthest east, or realm
        Of Persian Cyrus, or by factious Don.

The issues of the Future a wise God
Veils in the dark impenetrable Night,
    And smiles if mortals stretch
        Care beyond bounds to mortal minds assigned.

That which is present heed, and justly weigh;
All else flows onward as the river runs—
    Now, in mid-channel calm,
        Peacefully gliding to Etruscan seas;

Now, when wild torrents chafe its quiet streams,
Rolling, along with its resistless rush,
    Loosed crags, uprooted trees,
        And herds and flocks, and the lost homes of men,

While neighbouring forests, and far mountain-peaks
Mingle their roar. Happy indeed is he,
    Lord of himself, to whom
        'Tis given to say, as each day ends, 'I have lived.'

To-morrow let the Sire invest the heaven
With darkest cloud or 'purest ray serene,'
    He mars not what has been,
        Nor from Time's sum blots out one fleeted hour.

CONDITION OR SITUATION:

Appreciating the Power of Poetry

PRESCRIPTION:

Dis Poetry (1992)

by Benjamin Zephaniah

Benjamin Zephaniah's 'Dis Poetry' is a vibrant celebration of poetry's accessibility and revolutionary power. Written in Caribbean dialect, the poem rejects elitist notions that poetry belongs only to academics or the privileged, asserting instead that poetry lives everywhere – on the streets, in music, in everyday speech.

Zephaniah emphasizes poetry's oral tradition and its role as a tool for social change and political resistance. The repetitive refrain 'Dis poetry' creates a rhythmic, performance-driven quality that embodies the poem's message: poetry should be heard, felt and experienced, not just read. The central theme champions poetry as a democratic art form that gives voice to the marginalized, challenges authority, and speaks truth to power. Zephaniah ultimately presents poetry as a living, breathing force that belongs to the people and serves as both entertainment and enlightenment.

Dis poetry is like a riddim dat drops
De tongue fires a riddim dat shoots like shots
Dis poetry is designed fe rantin
Dance hall style, big mouth chanting,
Dis poetry nar put yu to sleep
Preaching follow me
Like yu is blind sheep,
Dis poetry is not Party Political
Not designed fe dose who are critical.
Dis poetry is wid me when I gu to me bed
It gets into me dreadlocks
It lingers around me head
Dis poetry goes wid me as I pedal me bike
I've tried Shakespeare, respect due dere
But did is de stuff I like.

Dis poetry is not afraid of going ina book
Still dis poetry need ears fe hear an eyes fe hav a look
Dis poetry is Verbal Riddim, no big words involved
An if I hav a problem de riddim gets it solved,
I've tried to be more romantic, it does nu good for me
So I tek a Reggae Riddim an build me poetry,
I could try be more personal
But you've heard it all before,

Pages of written words not needed
Brain has many words in store,
Yu could call dis poetry Dub Ranting
De tongue plays a beat
De body starts skanking,
Dis poetry is quick an childish
Dis poetry is fe de wise an foolish,
Anybody can do it fe free,
Dis poetry is fe yu an me,
Don't stretch yu imagination
Dis poetry is fe de good of de Nation,
Chant,
In de morning
I chant
In de night
I chant
In de darkness
An under de spotlight,
I pass thru University
I pass thru Sociology
An den I got a dread degree
In Dreadfull Ghettology.

Dis poetry stays wid me when I run or walk
An when I am talking to meself in poetry I talk,
Dis poetry is wid me,
Below me an above,
Dis poetry's from inside me
It goes to yu
WID LUV.

List of Poets and Poems

Adcock, Fleur, 'Things', p. 117
Agard, John, 'Diversity in de Market', p. 178
Akhmatova, Anna, 'The Sentence', p. 68
Armitage, Simon, 'You're Beautiful', p. 167
Arnold, Matthew, 'Growing Old', p. 138
Auden, W. H., 'Funeral Blues', p. 61
Barrett Browning, Elizabeth, 'Work', p. 119
Baudelaire, Charles, 'Intoxication', p. 194
Beckett, Samuel, 'Cascando', p. 100
Betjeman, John, 'Executive', p. 187
Bishop, Elizabeth, 'One Art', p. 50
Blake, William, 'A Poison Tree', p. 92
Brontë, Anne, 'Lines Composed in a Wood on a Windy Day', p. 64
Brontë, Charlotte, 'Life', p. 192
Brontë, Emily, 'Hope', p. 94
Brooke, Rupert, 'The Treasure', p. 118
Browning, Robert, 'Meeting at Night', p. 24
Bukowski, Charles, 'Roll the Dice', p. 184
Burns, Robert, 'A Red, Red Rose', p. 32
Byron, George Gordon, 'When We Two Parted', p. 16
Clare, John, 'First Love', p. 18
Cleary, Brendan, 'Lasagne', p. 114
Coleridge, Samuel Taylor, 'Kubla Khan', p. 123
Coolidge, Susan, 'A Lonely Moment', p. 157
Cope, Wendy, 'Spared', p. 160
Cowper, William, 'The Jackdaw', p. 79
Creeley, Robert, 'Oh', p. 146

Day-Lewis, Cecil, 'Walking Away', p. 144
Dickinson, Emily, 'Hope Is the Thing with Feathers', p. 63
Donne, John, 'No Man Is an Island', p. 132
Dowson, Ernest, 'You Would Have Understood Me, Had You Waited', p. 40
Dryden, John, 'Farewell Ungrateful Traitor', p. 44
Duffy, Carol Ann, 'We Remember Your Childhood Well', p. 90
Ehrmann, Max, 'Desiderata', p. 210
Eliot, George, 'Count That Day Lost', p. 209
Eliot, T. S., 'The Hollow Men', p. 71
Frost, Robert, 'The Road Not Taken', p. 180
García Lorca, Federico, 'The Faithless Wife', p. 29
Ginsberg, Allen, 'Velocity of Money', p. 206
von Goethe, Johann Wolfgang, 'Restless Love', p. 10
Graves, Robert, 'Down, Wanton, Down!', p. 110
Hafiz, 'Beauty Is a Waving Tree', p. 53
Hardy, Thomas, 'Between Us Now', p. 42
Hopkins, Gerard Manley, 'The Windhover', p. 66
Horace, 'Odes 3:29', p. 213
Hughes, Frieda, 'Stonepicker', p. 103
Hughes, Langston, 'As I Grew Older', p. 96
Jonson, Ben, 'Doing, a Filthy Pleasure Is, and Short', p. 164

Joyce, James, 'At That Hour', p. 191
Kavanagh, Patrick, 'On Raglan Road', p. 20
Kay, Jackie, 'Keeping Orchids', p. 121
Keats, John, 'To Autumn', p. 201
Kipling, Rudyard, 'If', p. 176
Lawrence, D. H., 'Intimates', p. 27
Mandelstam, Osip, 'I Was a Child in the World of the Powerful', p. 140
de la Mare, Walter, 'Good-bye', p. 78
Marlowe, Christopher, 'Who Ever Loved That Loved Not at First Sight', p. 22
Marvell, Andrew, 'The Definition of Love', p. 37
Mayakovsky, Vladimir, 'Listen!', p. 149
Meynell, Alice, 'Renouncement', p. 46
Milton, John, 'On His Blindness', p. 84
Moore, Thomas, 'An Argument', p. 151
Naidu, Sarojini, 'Cradle Song', p. 155
Neruda, Pablo, 'Here I Love You', p. 12
Nichols, Grace, 'Price We Pay for the Sun', p. 165
Nye, Naomi Shihab, 'Mediterranean Blue', p. 148
Owen, Wilfred, 'Futility', p. 55
Parker, Dorothy, 'A Dream Lies Dead', p. 104
Pasternak, Boris, 'February', p. 112
Patten, Brian, 'Party Piece', p. 172
Piñero, Miguel, 'La Bodega Sold Dreams', p. 204
Plath, Sylvia, 'A Life', p. 107
Poe, Edgar Allan, 'A Dream Within a Dream', p. 189
Pope, Alexander, 'Ode on Solitude', p. 85
Pushkin, Alexander, 'Consolation', p. 196
Rimbaud, Arthur, 'The Sleeper in the Valley', p. 82
Roethke, Theodore, 'In a Dark Time', p. 74
Rossetti, Christina, 'Remember', p. 52
Rossetti, Dante Gabriel, 'Sudden Light', p. 115
Schiller, Friedrich, 'The Conflict', p. 142
Scott, Walter, 'An Hour with Thee', p. 34
Shakespeare, William, 'All the World's a Stage', p. 69
Shelley, Percy Bysshe, 'Ozymandias', p. 98
Smith, Stevie, 'Not Waving but Drowning', p. 136
Soyinka, Wole, 'Telephone Conversation', p. 199
Stevens, Wallace, 'Thirteen Ways of Looking at a Blackbird', p. 127
Swinburne, Algernon Charles, 'A Leave-Taking', p. 8
Tagore, Rabindranath, 'Where the Mind is Without Fear', p. 134
Teasdale, Sara, 'Stars', p. 76
Tennyson, Alfred, 'Come Not, When I Am Dead', p. 14
Thomas, Dylan, 'Do Not Go Gentle into That Good Night', p. 59
Thomas, Edward, 'The Owl', p. 162
Tolkien, J. R. R., 'I Sit Beside the Fire and Think', p. 106
Tsvetaeva, Marina, 'Girlfriend', p. 25
Tyutchev, Fyodor, 'The Last Love', p. 36
Whitman, Walt, 'O Captain! My Captain!', p. 57
Wilde, Oscar, 'Sonnet to Liberty', p. 153
Wordsworth, William, 'The World Is Too Much with Us', p. 197
Yeats, W. B., 'The Lake Isle of Innisfree', p. 182
Zephaniah, Benjamin, 'Dis Poetry', p. 216

Acknowledgments

I would like to thank for the following people for their fantastic work on getting this anthology in shape. Firstly, Nicki Crossley, my editor at Michael O'Mara Books, for suggesting the project in the first place and for her enduring patience, and Vicky Bywater for doing such a great job and bringing it all together. I also wish to thank Barbara Ward, Gabby Smith, Vincent Camacho and Lucy Stewardson for their hard work and dedication. A special mention to my partner Rosa for her kind encouragement and emotional support and, lastly, I would like to thank all the poets, past and present, for their healing words of solace and therapeutic food for thought.

Credits

The author and publisher are grateful to the following for permission to use material that is in copyright:

Fleur Adcock: 'Things', from *Collected Poems* (Bloodaxe Books, 2024). Reproduced with permission of Bloodaxe Books.

John Agard: 'Diversity in de Market', from *Border Zone* (Bloodaxe Books, 2022). Reproduced with permission of Bloodaxe Books.

Anna Akhmatova: 'The Sentence', from *The Complete Poems of Anna Akhmatova*, translated by J. Hemschemeyer, edited and introduced by R. Reeder. Copyright © 1989, 1992, 1997 by J. Hemschemeyer. Reprinted by permission of The Permissions Company, LLC on behalf of Zephyr Press, zephyrpress.org (US) and by permission of Canongate Books (UK).

Simon Armitage: 'You're Beautiful', from *Tyrannosaurus Rex Versus the Corduroy Kid* (UK: Faber & Faber, 2006). And in the US: "You're Beautiful" from *The Shout: Selected Poems* by Simon Armitage. Used by permission of Alfred A. Knopf, an imprint of the Knopf Doubleday Publishing Group, a division of Penguin Random House LLC. All rights reserved. Copyright © 2005 by Simon Armitage.

W. H. Auden: 'Funeral Blues', from *Another Time* (Random House, 1940). Copyright © 1940 by The Estate of W. H. Auden. Reprinted by permission of Curtis Brown, Ltd., US. All rights reserved.

'Funeral Blues', copyright 1940 and © renewed 1968 by W. H. Auden; from *Collected Poems* by W. H. Auden, edited by Edward Mendelson. Used by permission of Random House, an imprint and division of Penguin Random House LLC, UK. All rights reserved.

Samuel Beckett: 'Cascando', from *The Complete Dramatic Works* (UK: Faber & Faber, 2006)(US: Grove Press, 2006). Reprinted by permission of Faber & Faber Ltd.

John Betjeman: 'Executive', from *Collected Poems* by John Betjeman (UK: John Murray, 1958)(US: Farrar, Straus and Giroux, 2006). Copyright © 2006 by The Estate of John Betjeman, Introduction Copyright © 2006 by Andrew Motion. Reprinted by permission of Farrar, Straus and Giroux. All Rights Reserved.

Elizabeth Bishop: 'One Art', from *Poems* by Elizabeth Bishop published by Chatto & Windus. Copyright © The Alice H. Methfessel Trust, 2011. Reprinted by permission of The Random House Group Limited, UK. Publisher's Note and compilation copyright © 2011 by Farrar, Straus and Giroux. Reprinted by permission of Farrar, Straus and Giroux, US. All Rights Reserved.

Charles Bukowski: 'Roll the Dice', from *Essential Bukowski Poetry* by C. Bukowski (HarperCollins, 2016). Copyright © 2016 by Linda Lee Bukowski.

Brendan Cleary: 'Lasagne'. Copyright © Brendan Cleary. Reprinted by permission of Brendan Cleary.

Wendy Cope: 'Spared', from *Collected Poems* (Faber & Faber, 2024).Copyright © Wendy Cope 2001. Reprinted by permission of Faber & Faber Ltd.

Robert Creeley: 'Oh', from *Selected Poems of Robert Creeley, 1945–2005*. Copyright © The Regents of the University of California, 1996. Reprinted by permission of University of California Press.

Elizabeth Daryush: 'Poem 13', from *Sonnets From Hafez & other verses*, published in *Selected Poems* (Carcanet, 1997). Reprinted by permission of Carcanet Press Ltd.

Cecil Day-Lewis: 'Walking Away', from *Complete Poems* by C. Day-Lewis, published by Sinclair Stevenson. Copyright © C. Day-Lewis, 1992. Reprinted by permission of The Random House Group Limited.

Carol Ann Duffy: 'We Remember Your Childhood Well', from *The Other Country* by C. A. Duffy. Published by Anvil Press Poetry, 1990. Copyright © C. A. Duffy. Reproduced by permission of the author c/o Rogers, Coleridge & White Ltd., 20 Powis Mews, London W11 1JN.

T. S. Eliot: 'The Hollow Men', from *Collected Poems 1909–1962* (Faber & Faber, 2002). Reprinted by permission of Faber & Faber Ltd.

Federico García Lorca: 'The Faithless Wife', from *Selected Poems*, translated by Merryn Williams (Bloodaxe Books, 1992). Reproduced with permission of Bloodaxe Books.

Allen Ginsberg: 'Velocity of Money' poem by Allen Ginsberg. Copyright © Allen Ginsberg, 1994, used by permission of The Wylie Agency (UK) Limited. And from *Collected Poems 1947–1997* by Allen Ginsberg (US: HarperCollins, 2007).

Robert Graves: 'Down, Wanton, Down!', from *Complete Poems Vol I* (Carcanet, 2000). Reprinted by permission of Carcanet Press Ltd.

Frieda Hughes: 'Stonepicker', from *Out of the Ashes* (Bloodaxe Books, 2018). Reproduced with permission of Bloodaxe Books.

Patrick Kavanagh: 'On Raglan Road', is reprinted from *Collected Poems*, edited by Antoinette Quinn (Allen Lane, 2004), by kind permission of the Trustees of the Estate of the late Katherine B. Kavanagh, through the Jonathan Williams Literary Agency.

Jackie Kay: 'Keeping Orchids', from *Darling: New & Selected Poems* (Bloodaxe Books, 2007). Reproduced with permission of Bloodaxe Books.

D. H. Lawrence: 'Intimates', from *The Cambridge Edition of the Works of DH Lawrence: Poems, volume 1*. Copyright © Cambridge University Press 2013. Reproduced by permission of Paper Lion Ltd, The Estate of Frieda Lawrence Ravagli and Cambridge University Press.

Osip Mandelstam: 'I Was a Child in the World of the Powerful', from *The Moscow & Voronezh Notebooks, Poems 1930–1937*, tr. by Richard and Elizabeth McKane (Bloodaxe Books, 2003). Reproduced with permission of Bloodaxe Books.

Walter de la Mare: 'Good-bye', from *The Veil and Other Poems* (Constable, 1921). Reprinted by permission of the Society of Authors.

Vladimir Mayakovsky: 'Listen!', from *Listen!: Early Poems 1913–1918*, translated by Maria Enzensberger (Redstone, 1987). Reprinted by permission of Redstone Press Ltd.

Pablo Neruda: 'Here I Love You', from *Twenty Love Poems and a Song of Despair* by Pablo Neruda, published by Jonathan Cape. Copyright © Pablo Neruda, 1969. English translation copyright © W. S. Merwin, 1969. Reprinted by permission of The Random House Group Limited.

Grace Nichols: 'Price We Pay for the Sun', from *The Fat Black Woman's Poems* (Virago, 1984), copyright © Grace Nichols 1984. Reprinted with permissions from Curtis Brown Group Ltd on behalf of Grace Nichols.

Naomi Shihab Nye: 'Mediterranean Blue', from *The Tiny Journalist*. Copyright © 2019 Naomi Shihab Nye. Reprinted with the permission of The Permissions Company, LLC on behalf of BOA Editions, Ltd., boaeditions.org.

Boris Pasternak: 'February', from *Poems of Boris Pasternak*, chosen and translated by Lydia Pasternak Slater (Unwin Paperbacks, 1963 and expanded ed in 1984). Reprinted by permission of The Pasternak Trust.

Brian Patten: 'Party Piece', from *The Mersey Sound* (Penguin, 1967). Copyright Brian Patten 1967.

Miguel Piñero: 'La Bodega Sold Dreams', from *Outlaw: The Collected Works of Miguel Piñero* (Arte Público Press, 2010). 41 Lines reprinted with permission from the publisher (© 2010 Arte Público Press, University of Houston).

Sylvia Plath: 'A Life', from *Collected Poems* (UK: Faber & Faber, 1981) and from *The Collected Poems* (US: HarperCollins, 2008). Reprinted by permission of Faber & Faber Ltd.

Theodore Roethke: 'In a Dark Time', from *Collected Poems of Theodore Roethke* (Faber & Faber, 1985). Copyright © Beatrice Roethke, 1963.

Stevie Smith: 'Not Waving But Drowning', from *Collected Poems of Stevie Smith*. Copyright © 1972 by Stevie Smith. Reprinted with the permission of The Permissions Company, LLC, US, on behalf of New Directions Publishing Corp., ndbooks.com; and from *Collected Poems and Drawings by Stevie Smith* (UK: Faber & Faber Ltd, 2018). Reprinted by permission of Faber & Faber Ltd.

Wole Soyinka: 'Telephone Conversation', from *Modern Poetry From Africa* (Penguin Books, 1963), edited by Gerald Moore and Ulli Beier. Copyright © Wole Soyinka, 1963.

Dylan Thomas: 'Do Not Go Gentle into That Good Night', from *The Poems of Dylan Thomas*. Copyright ©1952 by Dylan Thomas. Reprinted by permission of New Directions Publishing Corp. (US)

J. R. R. Tolkien: 'I Sit Beside the Fire and Think', from *The Fellowship of the Ring* (George Allen & Unwin, 1954). Copyright © The Tolkien Estate Ltd 1954, 1966.

Marina Tsvetaeva: 'Girlfriend', from *Bride of Ice: New Selected Poems*, translated by Elaine Feinstein (Carcanet, 2023). Reprinted with the permission of Carcanet Press Ltd.

Fyodor Tyutchev: 'Last Love', from *Fyodor Tyutchev – Selected Poems*, translated by John Dewey (Brimstone Press, 2014). Reprinted with the permission of Brimstone Press Ltd.

Benjamin Zephaniah: 'Dis Poetry', from *Dis Poetry: Selected Poems & Lyrics*, (Bloodaxe Books, 2025). Reproduced with permission of Bloodaxe Books.

References:

allpoetry.com; bloodaxebooks.com @bloodaxebooks (X/facebook) #bloodaxebooks; archive.org; gutenberg.org; poetryfoundation.org; poetryinternational.com; scottishpoetrylibrary.org.uk